Control What You Can Control

Control What You Can Control

A Path to Happiness

Robert Pawlicki Ph.D.

ISBN-13: 9781544191614
ISBN-10: 1544191618

Also by Robert Pawlicki, Ph.D.

Success By Another Measure: Recognizing and enhancing your character
Fifty Ways to Greater Well Being and Happiness: A handy and
inspirational guide

Our life is the creation of our mind.

BUDDHA

The whole universe is change and life itself is what you deem it.

MARCUS AURELIUS

The mind is its own place, and in itself, can make heaven of hell, and a hell of heaven.

JOHN MILTON

Most people are about as happy as they make up their minds to be.

ABRAHAM LINCOLN

To my daughters, Heather and Lisa

Table of Contents

Exercises to Control What You Can Control and to Create Your Path to Happiness

Preface

THERE IS A man on death row whom many describe as evil incarnate. A convicted serial killer and rapist, his life has been filled with endless violent and disgusting crimes. When asked why he is this way, he answers quickly and with certainty, "My father made me who I am. Every day of my childhood he beat me mercilessly."

Less than fifty miles away, in a little rural town lives another man, the same age as our prisoner. He, however, has lived a life of rectitude. He has been the mayor for most of his adult life, as well as the town's church and community leader. His town people would vouch that he is the most kind, generous, and sensitive person they know. It seems his goodness knows no bounds. When asked why he is the way he is, he too answers, "My father made me who I am. Every day of my childhood he beat me mercilessly." It turns out that these two men are twin brothers.

This somewhat apocryphal story first came to my attention almost 30-years ago in reading an early book by the motivational speaker, Anthony Robbins. It turns out, however, not to be as theoretical as I first thought. I have subsequently come across several cases of siblings whose lives, despite significant biological and environment similarities, are diametrically different. The startling contrast between brothers or sisters betrays our assumption that childhood dictates behavior. Perhaps the adage, "as the twig is bent so grows the tree," needs to be reconsidered. How the individual perceives and interprets the experiences of life may be more crucial than simply the experiences he or she has. It appears that what each of us decides to do with what we experience determines what our life becomes. Our lives are more under our control than we often assume. This assumption drives the thoughts in this book. What we do with what we experience determines our happiness.

Why did you picked up a book on happiness? You may simply be a lover of self-help books, and the title sounds like a useful guide, which it is. Maybe you have some long-standing issue or general stress and have considered therapy, but are not quite ready to take the plunge. Perhaps you feel a need to independently master your own issues, and therapy implies failure. Maybe you feel a general malaise that has been lingering for a while. Or you may be interested in professional help, but the cost or other inconveniences are a deterrent.

What do you do when you feel bad physically? I'm sure you have well-practiced habits: get a good night sleep, perhaps take some over-the-counter medicine, or re-arrange your schedule. If the symptoms get worse or go on for a while, you reluctantly give in and see a physician. This pattern is well established for many people.

However, for those who experience psychological and emotional distress, the pattern is different. Because our emotional state is intertwined with our sense of self and character, the path before seeking professional help is more complicated. Depending on our background and the problem, we may hope it goes away or resolves of its own accord. We may blame others, or luck, or believe there is nothing to be done — "It is what it is." We may believe that we are inadequate or inferior in some way, but don't want to deal with these feelings. We may turn to excessive work, alcohol, drugs or other addictions to keep our problems in the background.

In the meantime we ruminate, fret, worry, avoid, blame, and numerous other actions that fail to move us toward constructive outcomes. Certainly if we feel *continually* stressed, unhappy, inferior, sad or angry, our efforts are not working. The oft-quoted premise,

"The definition of insanity is doing the same thing over and over and expecting different results" is appropriate here. An intelligent alternative, therefore, is to search out different answers and be open to trying them.

Without doubt, for those whose issues are life threatening or significantly intruding upon everyday life, medical help and psychotherapy is the smartest choice. Those, however, who are not ready for therapy, may find this book an aid to creating a personal path to get unstuck, and on the path to greater happiness.

There are 57 chapters in this book, purposely short and easy to understand. So short that each can be read in a matter of minutes. Twenty-four of the chapters have associated exercises that I believe are critical to making progress. In my over 30 years of providing therapy, each of my clients has heard the same mantra:[1]

I'm here to listen carefully, to fully understand your circumstances and issues. I'm here as a partner in helping you to significantly lessen your problem(s), to work to create a plan with you so that you may approach your difficulties in a new constructive fashion. I am here, not simply to help resolve your current problem, but to teach you techniques that can help you in the future. What I cannot do is practice new behaviors and thinking for you.

In my experience, the techniques and ideas discussed in these chapters have a very high rate of success in facilitating change *when* clients commit themselves to practicing the techniques and ideas that we discuss.

Fans of my previous books say that the content is enjoyable to read, but change doesn't come about for most people simply as a

---

1 Patient confidentiality, of course, is paramount and protected by the modifications of their identity.

result of reading. You may be the exception, but the scientific research shows that for the majority of individuals, it takes more. In book form it takes doing the exercises, as simple as they may sometimes seem, that will help you implement the ideas and direct your personal path to a happier life.

The book is so straightforward that you can read it in one sitting. I don't recommend it. If you do, count it as the first of many readings, with the majority of times going back to specific sections that you find most relevant to your issues. Carefully consider the material and do the exercises. Many of the exercises, such as those on kindness and gratitude are *fun*, as more than one client has reported.

We *all* have behaviors and emotions that go astray. The critical variable is to learn patterns that avoid difficulties and to acquire skills to abbreviate these issues when they occur -- and they will occur. There are numerous ways to truncate a bad behavior, mood, sadness, anxiety and other trying emotions. This book is a guide to do just that. It lays out the work that needs to be done to travel the path to happiness. It is this work that must be done to create a life that is generally mentally healthy and happy — just as we must exercise and eat well to maintain a healthy body.

One way to use this book is to read a chapter at bedtime. In fact, I gave serious consideration to using the title, *Bedside Happiness, Ideas to ponder while you sleep*. It's a marvelous way to put inspirational and constructive thoughts in your mind. It also interferes with the habit of ruminating over the stresses of the day at bedtime and may help you begin a plan to improve upon some long-standing problem. Hope and optimism are wonderfully medicinal during sleep.

Many of us have a natural proclivity to focus on the negative. The positive takes work. We are also inclined to see outside factors such as luck, circumstances, other people, etc. as the cause of our distress, while placing our own actions in the shadows. Or, as is often the case, we place blame on our own actions in a damning, self-deprecating fashion that does little to resolve our issues. These patterns and perceptions are at the heart of the pages that lie ahead.

So welcome to my world of good mental health, general happiness and well being. Read, contemplate and actually practice what is recommended. It will be well worth your effort.[2]

Robert Pawlicki, Ph.D.
Savannah, Georgia

---

2 Eight chapters from my book, *Fifty Ways to Greater Well Being and Happiness*, are included in Section one. I believe they are fundamental to establishing the foundation of happiness and essential in cementing the assumption that your happiness is a choice dictated by your thinking.

Those readers who have read, *Fifty Ways to Greater Well Being and Happiness* may want to skip section one. I, however, do recommend rereading them. I'm the author and I reread them when I'm feeling distressed or just need a reminder of good mental health practices.

Overview of Section 1

Control What You Can Control

"You've never seen a boss like mine. I can't begin to tell you how erratic he is."

"It's my daughter. She's driving me crazy."

"My husband is a Neanderthal. No doubt about it. He's from another age."

These are the types of statements psychologists and therapists hear on a regular basis. In all cases they are true — partially. Partially, in the sense that outside factors always have an influence upon us to some degree. A critical issue in maintaining our own happiness, however, is whether we take charge of our own response to the upsetting behavior. It is whether we control what we can control that determines the degree that we are "driven crazy" by someone or something else.

It is this critical element, controlling what you can control, that is at the heart of most modern therapeutic interventions. When the patient has a 35-year-old addicted daughter, it's not the daughter that can be changed by the therapist. Nor the outlandish boss or the crude, lazy husband. The patient must change what the patient controls.

The same holds true outside of therapy in everyday life. In each case, and in virtually every constructive problem-solving situation, the effort revolves around a clarification of the issue, and an understanding of what can be done and not done by each of us. In other words, what is under our control and what is not?

1

CHAPTER 1

Control What You Can Control: What alternative do you have?

ABOUT FIFTEEN YEARS ago I conducted a series of lectures and discussions in two state prisons.[3] Walking into a maximum-security prison is an incredible experience. Your television images are probably somewhat accurate — the harsh, cold, dehumanizing environment and the incredibly small cells are there before your eyes. What you cannot fully sense on your television set is the daily fear, the lack of privacy, the constant noise, the loneliness and the danger. Men in this severe environment vary widely in their ability to cope. Most remarkably, some are happy — happier than at any other time in their lives.[4] I repeatedly asked prisoners, "Is it possible to be happy in prison?" I never heard any prisoner say no, even though everyone said it was difficult.

· When I share this information, surprise is the most common reaction. The loss of freedom in the austere dangerous prison environment, void of the people and things we love, seems a hardship unbearable to manage. And yet this most harsh existence is, for some, a place where satisfaction is found. The men who were the most successful had found a little niche that they could control in a sea of experiences beyond their control.

---

3 Lebanon and Warren Correctional Institutes
4 One prisoner, highly admired for his basketball skills behind walls, clearly reported feeling happier in prison than outside.

Most prisoners were not happy, but some were, and others were happier than they had been outside of prison. Once again, the point being that so much of happiness has to do with our internal dialog.

There are many, many people who make their own prison, with walls created of fear, anxiety or depression. These emotions, typically fueled by distorted thinking, limit constructive behavior, because they interfere with problem solving. Whether it's a health, relationship, financial or the myriad of other problems that are a part of life's struggles, an early question in managing debilitating emotions should be "What part of this situation can I control?" Among the many benefits of asking this question is that it takes us away from one of the most destructive ways of approaching personal problems — blaming.

Blaming is seductive, for it often comes with a benefit — a temporary avoidance of looking at our responsibility in the situation. This temporary advantage comes at a substantial cost, however. It puts constructive problem solving out of our control and control into the hands of others — often the very people we would least like to be in charge of our emotional state. Blaming also creates anger, rarely a favorable emotion, as well as interfering with moving onto more pleasant endeavors.

It's interesting to remind ourselves of the stories that we hear of people facing incredible hardships. When we analyze how these heroic individuals have not only survived but also have thrived, we realize that their internal dialog is not filled with blame or regret. Like the oft-cited Serenity Prayer, they took some of life's most extreme challenges, accepted the part they couldn't control and worked on controlling what they could. It is a lesson that we need to remind ourselves of, day after day after day. Move away from blame, control what you can control — a major step in creating a happier life.

The Serenity Prayer

God grant me the serenity to accept the things I cannot change; courage to change the things I can; and wisdom to know the difference.

Reinhold Niebuhr

Exercise
Create Your Path: Control what you can control

List your two most vexing problems.

1.

2.

For each of these, list what you can control and what you cannot.

Problem 1

Can control	Cannot control
1.	1.
2.	2.
3.	3.

Problem 2

Can control	Cannot control
1.	1.
2.	2.
3.	3.

CHAPTER 2

Beliefs: The power to do good or harm

A MAN WHO was treated in our clinic literally took ten minutes to walk across a room.[5] His difficulty was an erroneous belief that "if I move too fast my spine will crumble." Our team was very successful in altering his condition — so much so, that in three weeks he was walking ten miles a day as measured by a pedometer! How did we do it? We performed what I call a "belief-ectomy," that is, we removed his belief.

Our own beliefs, often reflected in our general philosophy of life, are very powerful. They can cause great good or harm.

Strangely, most of us have a difficult time articulating this driving force in our lives. Our basic beliefs have often been relegated to the back of our minds, subject to a difficult, searching recall. It's understandable. The issues and pressures of daily life take precedence.

But beliefs are fundamental building blocks of our identity. They play a critical role in determining the direction of our lives. Take one patient I saw many years ago who adamantly claimed that "He who dies with the most toys wins." Still another believed "I can't fail in my father's eyes." Then there are others, like a friend who believes "My life would be lost if I didn't volunteer." You can easily

---

5 For 20 of my over 35 years of providing clinical therapy, I was either a member or director of multidisciplinary chronic pain programs at the West Virginia University and the University of Cincinnati Medical Centers.

see how each belief, passionately held, could significantly influence the direction and well being of a person.

There are some belief categories that are especially egregious to mental well being: beliefs that harbor blame — "My misery is a result of" -– fill in the blank. Other beliefs teem with prejudice — "The poor or rich or minority group is the cause of all of our troubles. The government, big business is going to be the death of us all." Beliefs that view the world in black and white — "You're either my friend or my enemy." Beliefs that look at the world as highly threatening — "You never know when someone is going deceive you." or cynical — "People are basically untrustworthy".

On the other hand, when beliefs have a positive tone, they are much more likely to reside in a happier and more secure individual. Examples abound: Generosity — "In spite of their flaws, people are basically decent." Optimism — "I continue to believe that I will land on my feet." Perspective — "I've been through all kinds of adversity. I'll have more good fortune in the future. I can handle it." — Complexity "Even people I don't agree with can be good and fair-minded."

Beliefs can be incredibly stubborn. There is a story told by Abraham Maslow that illustrates the point. According to Maslow, a psychiatrist was treating a patient who believed that he was a corpse. In spite of the psychiatrist's best logic and effort, the patient continued with his bizarre perception. In desperation the psychiatrist asked the patient, "Do corpses bleed?" "That's absurd," replied the patient, "Corpses do not bleed." After getting the patient's permission, the psychiatrist proceeded to prick the man's finger with a pin, producing a drop of blood. Staring at the blood for a moment, the patient turned to the psychiatrist and exclaimed, "I'll be damned. Corpses do bleed!" This resistance to reality is common.

Although the psychiatrist was unsuccessful in persuading the patient, he was on the right track. Introducing doubt can change beliefs, and doubt comes from an examination of alternative thoughts. In the case of the clinic patient mentioned earlier, the removal of his old belief occurred because we slowly but safely demonstrated that movement was not going to cause his spine to crumble.

When we realize that some of our personal beliefs are harmful to our well being we can take action to change the situation. Obviously, as a retired psychologist, I believe seeking the assistance of an outside professional is a valuable option. But openness with friends and loved ones is another alternative. The critical element is a willingness to consider opposing evidence, always a challenge. In light of just how important beliefs are to our well being, it certainly seems worth the effort.

CHAPTER 3

Thinking Makes It So

YOU WOULD BE hard pressed to persuade most people that events in their lives have little to do with their happiness. But that's what most experts conclude — events have very little to do with happiness. And it's not just modern research on well being that has come to that conclusion. It's evident in the writings of the great sages in world history. In the Far East, Buddha suggested, "Our life is the creation of our mind." The famous Greek philosopher, Marcus Aurelius, wrote, "The whole universe is change and life itself is but what you deem it." During the Renaissance John Milton argued, "The mind is its own place, and in itself, can make Heaven of Hell, and a Hell of Heaven."

In modern Cognitive Behavioral Therapy, a form of psychotherapy, the basic assumption is, "It's not the events of the world, it's your interpretation of the events that create your emotions." Why is it that both science and the great thinkers of the world believe that events are not the drivers of happiness?

I often ask the following question in working with clients: "Is there another person who has remarkably similar circumstances to you and is happy?" The clients, typically and begrudgingly, admit that someone else may have a difficult husband, wife, boss, or relative or is suffering significant financial loss, or is even experiencing chronic pain, but is happier than they. With that answer we can loosen up the belief that their particular situation *always* causes misery. We can begin to make progress in reducing the stranglehold that misery has on a person. We can then discuss what it is that differs between one person and another in roughly the same situation. The answer inevitably becomes how we interpret the situation, just as the philosophers through the ages have noted.

If you doubt the above, consider the following: Michael J. Fox, was diagnosed with Parkinson's disease at the age of 29, and at the height of his starring role in the popular television series, *Family Ties*. Such an occurrence could be perceived as a life tragedy but Michael J. Fox viewed it differently. In his memoir, "Lucky Man," he states it like this:

> "The ten years since my diagnosis have been the best ten years of my life, and I consider myself a lucky man."

He did he not succumb to the challenges of a chronic intrusive ailment. Instead he established the Michael J. Fox Foundation for Parkinson's research and continues his television career to this day. Not everyone can be as heroic as Michael J. Fox, but we can all learn that it is our thinking and controlling what we can control, that is at the heart of our well being.[6]

Accepting that a person's thinking about an event is a critical variable doesn't, however, change how they perceive things. It's just a starting point. However, if I accept that my interpretation, my perception, is tied to my emotional state, then I can at least be open to a discussion. If, on the other hand, I believe that my anger, depression, anxiety, whatever, is entirely a result of someone or something else, then I'm at a dead end. Since others are mostly outside of my control, I have little realistic hope of changing my misery.

---

6 At age 56, he currently stars in a recurrent role on the popular television series, *The Good Wife*, where he has won Emmy nominations for the past three years.

The idea that the events around us are not the sole or critical factor controlling our happiness is a difficult concept to fully accept. After all, don't we feel happier when we are properly sheltered, fed, socially supported and sexually satisfied? Of course we do and, of course, we seek things that provide us with pleasure. None of the scientists or philosophers spoken of denies that we are hardwired to seek pleasure, in its myriad forms, and to avoid pain. Nevertheless, the filter through which we experience our positive and negative input, determines our emotional state. It is that filter, our individual perception that is so important.

So seek pleasure. Avoid pain. You have no choice but to do so. Even the masochist who loves to feel pain is an illustration of how our perceptions really dictate our experience. We all know that "one man pleasure is another man's pain." But always, always, recognize that it's your interpretation of what is happening around you that will rule your happiness. Such a belief frees a person from blaming others and thereby losing control. Accepting that your interpretation plays a critical role in your well being moves you into maturity and control. As Shakespeare said, "There is nothing either good or bad, but thinking makes it so."

CHAPTER 4

Where is Happiness Found?

MANY YEARS AGO a friend asked if I could chat with her about a problem. She had been widowed for three years after a long marriage and was now ready to begin a new life — but there was no one to begin her life with. My friend began her story by detailing the good, the bad and the ugly from her marriage, focusing mostly on the good, reporting few regrets but now ready to start anew. It was clear that she had done considerable work in moving through the grieving process and was comfortable with her memories.

The problem, as she saw it, was that she could not find a companion, and so there was emptiness in her life. It was not that she hadn't made an effort. Quite the contrary, she had tried singles groups, advertised in magazines (another era) and circulated in church settings, but found few opportunities. She was lonely. She wanted to share her life and feel the warmth of a companion.

She was perplexed because she had much to offer. She was a teacher and musician, worked at her physical fitness, was well spoken and quite engaging. However, in her mind, her life was not complete and would not be until she was a part of a matched pair.

I listened attentively, sympathized with her frustration, but then carefully began to challenge her assumption that her happiness was dependent upon finding a mate. She countered that she knew others who lived happily as singles, but she could not imagine doing so.

Exploring alternatives, she revealed that she had always wanted to travel to Europe, but family obligations had interfered. I gently pushed her to take charge of what she could control and to look inward, rather than allowing outside factors to control her happiness. My thoughts are well expressed in a favorite quote by Agnes Repplier,

> "It is not easy to find happiness in ourselves, and it is not possible to find it elsewhere."

To make a long story short, my friend went to Europe and had a great time, but more importantly, she began to change her belief that she could only be complete if she had a partner. An additional factor, a very critical one, is that my friend's vitality, her subtle message, had not been inviting. When she began to control her own life, however, her excitement returned and with it a quantum leap in confidence and attractiveness. Shortly thereafter, she did meet someone and has now been happily married for over ten years.

In her book, *"The How of Happiness,"* Sonja Lyubomirsky notes that,

> "Happy people are more likely to acquire lovers and friends"

and observes that,

> "Happiness will help you attract more and higher-quality relationships, which will make you even happier, and so on, in a continuous positive feedback loop."[7]

Interestingly, my friend shared my advice with a friend of hers, who then sought my counsel. She, too, had been widowed and was in the same early position, having searched out the "singles scene" and

---

7 Lyubomirsky, S., *The How of Happiness*, Penguin Press, New York, NY, 2007.

come up empty. Likewise, she had a great deal to offer, but could not find someone to share her life. Our conversation was similar in that I encouraged her to take control of her own happiness by managing her own beliefs and actions. She, too, came to exude a newfound energy, and a relationship soon appeared. Here's where the stories of my two advisees differ. Her new relationship did not last. She did not find a happily ever after story within a relationship. But she did find happiness within herself and continues to be dynamically different than the sad person I saw many years ago.

The true objective was not to find a partner. The real goal was to find happiness, and that can only be done by looking within, and controlling what you can, no matter the circumstances. It's not always an easy path to inner happiness, but as Agnes Repplier stated "it is not possible to find it elsewhere."

CHAPTER 5

It Is Your Moral Obligation to be Happy

Be good and you will be happy. We've heard that message all our lives, but the sequence is wrong. In fact, we are most good when we are happy. Think about it — when are you kindest? Probably when you are feeling happy. When you are feeling ebullient, you are likely your most "good," generous, charming, and delightful self. And, of course, the reverse is the case as well. When you are unhappy, depressed or miserable, you are self-centered, selfish and probably a curmudgeon, not a pleasant person to be around. Given this perspective, it can be logically argued that you have a moral obligation to be happy, for it is in this state that you will be the most kind to your fellow human beings.

Many people need permission to be happy. They believe they are not worthy, not deserving. They may have been indoctrinated with a childhood guilt that you have to be good before you can be happy. In reality they should have been taught it is important to be happy, and happiness will make it more likely that you will be good, kind and certainly more tolerant.

If we examine those who are very unhappy or depressed, we see the relationship between happiness and goodness even more clearly. Depression is a time of shutting down, turning inward. It is when problems become so dominant that the depressed person is unable to relate to others and has difficulty being compassionate. The person becomes inner focused. It is a time of depleted energy and changes in basic functions such as eating, sleeping, and concentration. Under such circumstances it is difficult for goodness to thrive, for goodness requires energy, compassion and empathy.

Depression, anger and blame narrow our focus. Anger reduces the field of thought and positive behavior. Blame, too, tends to restrict our energy, diverting it away from problem solving, compassion, kindness and creativity. Happiness, on the other hand, widens our scope and this expansiveness opens our world to greater sensitivity, awareness and generosity. Goodness, compassion and empathy are companions to happiness and when expressed, they generate additional rewards of their own.

Making happiness a priority is analogous to the instructions given by the airline personnel that, in an emergency, we place the oxygen mask over our own mouth before we tend to our children. If we place the mask on our child first and pass out from lack of oxygen, we can be of no benefit to our child. Whereas, if we place the mask over our own mouth first, we can revive a child who has momentarily passed out and later carry him or her to safety. What may initially strike us as selfish turns out to be smart — so too with taking care of our happiness. What appears on the surface to be selfish is, in fact, generous to those we love, for when we are happy we will provide those around us with greater kindness. Therefore, for the sake of others, it is our obligation to work at being happy.

CHAPTER 6

Choosing to be Happy

My wife, running, music, ice cream, my dog, kindness — these are the answers people give to the question, "What makes you happy?" The list goes on and on. It is rare for any of us not to have an answer of some sort. The question, "Are you happy?" however, is not so easily answered. People know what makes them happy, but they don't necessarily practice what they know.

Why the inconsistency? The answer may appear obvious. "I can't be happy when I've got to work, take care of my children, or worry about my finances. I'll be happy *after* I get a job, my loved one gets better, I pay off my credit cards." These answers embody the concerns of life that take priority over attention to happiness — even when we know what makes us happy. Understandable, perhaps, but nonetheless curious.

Desiring happiness is universal. Taking constructive action to become happy is not. And yet there are many experts who argue that happiness is a choice. To the distressed, however, there is no choice. Life's pressing problems take precedence.

Take Karen, a 41-year-old married woman, with two teenage boys, and a job as a computer programmer. Between a marriage that's gone stale, boys who create worry and havoc in her home, and her work that she doesn't particularly like, Karen doesn't feel the least bit happy. Karen knows what makes her happy — time with close friends, going to a Yoga class, and reading a good book. But ask Karen if she takes time to engage in these activities and you'll receive a staunch no. There's no time.

A critical question for Karen is this: Are there any other women, her age, in a stale marriage, with two teen boys, working in a job that they don't like, who are happier than she? If the answer is yes, the question then becomes what do these women do that Karen does not?

Fortunately, scientists have observed people who are able to thrive in difficult times. Here are a few of the characteristics that consistently show up:

1) The happier person continues to believe, in spite of difficult circumstances, that she has primary control of her life. Such a belief tends to provide an atmosphere that allows for constructive problem solving as opposed to despair.
2) The happier person arranges at least a small portion of each day to take care of her own needs, even in the face of pressing external demands. It may be as simple as doing a few minutes of exercise, going to a quiet relaxing space, or any other activity that is regularly incorporated into her day.
3) The happier person works at maintaining an optimistic attitude, retaining hope and perspective, and seeing the positive aspects within a difficult situation. Being aware of the positive details of life and regularly expressing gratitude for these things are aspects of this attitude.
4) The happier person uses a support system of friends or relatives to discuss the difficulties of her life.

When experts argue that happiness is a choice, they are not suggesting that difficulties disappear. Rather they are saying that we can look at things differently, even in difficult situations. Making sure the above recommendations are in place is a good place to start.

Notice that all of these things are within a person's control, although all require work to set in place. Traveling down the twisted path to happiness takes effort.

Exercise

Choose the Path You Take

Assess your own life to see how you measure up to what the experts believe is true of happy people. See if you can answer the following questions in the affirmative:

1. Do you believe that you are in control of your life? Do you take a small portion of each day to exclusively devote to your needs?
    a. If yes, wonderful. If no, write what you might change.

2. Do you maintain an optimistic attitude, even seeing the positive in difficult situations?
    a. If yes, wonderful. If no, write what you might change.

3. Do you express gratitude for those things you have?
    a. If yes, wonderful. If no, write what you might change.

4. And, perhaps most importantly, do you regularly share your life and concerns with friends and/or relatives?
    a. If yes, wonderful. If no, write what you might change.

CHAPTER 7

Acceptance: The path to a calmer life

THERE ARE MANY benefits in accepting those things that we cannot change. In our lifetime, every one of us has a parent, child or friendship that has driven us to distraction or worse. Perhaps it's someone's personal bad habits, bigotry, or opinionated manner. Whatever the source, we all know that certain behaviors can "drive us crazy," if we allow it. It is that last phrase — "if we allow it" — that is key. When we no longer allow it to affect us, but to a large degree accept that it is outside our control, we have moved to a higher level of maturity.

However, acceptance takes considerable effort and mental discipline, perhaps nowhere more so than accepting our own perceived deficiencies. Much of our life involves an inordinate amount of attention to what we perceive as our inadequacies. We may think ourselves too dumb, too short, too tall, too ugly, or . . . fill in the blank with your personal favorite.

Imagine how much energy we would save and how much happier we would be if we added a modicum of acceptance. Even better, imagine if we not only accepted the deficiency but also looked to our strengths to compensate for our weaknesses. Take Edward O. Wilson, Professor at Harvard University, winner of two Pulitzer prizes, and world-renowned naturalist. He writes this of himself:

"I am blind in one eye and cannot hear high frequency sounds; therefore I am an entomologist. I cannot memorize lines, have trouble visualizing words spelled out to me letter by letter, and am often unable to get digits in the right order while reading and copying numbers. So I contrived ways of expressing ideas that others can recite with quotations and formulas. This compensation is aided by an unusual ability to make comparisons of disparate objects, thus to produce syntheses of previously unconnected information. I write smoothly, in part I believe because my memory is less encumbered by the phrasing and nuances of others. I pushed these strengths and skirted the weaknesses."[8]

How many of us would have become victims or avoiders, filled with self-doubt, given the difficulties encountered by Edward O. Wilson? The trick may be, like Wilson, to spend less time devoted to our deficiencies and far more time attending to our strengths.

Look around in your own life. What are the things that you truly cannot do anything about and would be better off accepting? You might want to write out some self-deprecating thoughts and work to replace them with more constructive alternatives.

Try replacing "I've never been very smart" with "While I may have difficulty with math, I've have a remarkably good memory for details." I'm dumb or not very smart is a global label that doesn't fairly examine the breadth of your intelligence. It's a generalization that only does harm by encouraging self-pity and doubt.

Here's another example: You may blame yourself by thinking, "My son's life is a mess." You may then also be implicitly thinking, "and it's my fault." Such thoughts can be changed to "It's true that my son is having a difficult life. He has also had many bright spots in his life. I did the best I could under the circumstances, and now he has to make his own choices and live with the outcome." This more constructive interpretation would include the acceptance that your

---

8 Wilson, E.O., *Naturalist*, Island Press, Washington, D.C., 1994.

son has made his own choices, that many things were outside of your control, and that you are not responsible for your son's actions now. Focusing exclusively on the thought that your son's life is a mess is traveling on a path to frustration and sadness.

Acceptance is quite a challenge. But, if we put energy into meeting this challenge, the rewards are enormous.

Exercise

A Path to a Calmer life: Acceptance

1. Draw a line down the middle of a blank sheet of paper.

2. In the left column write down a recurring thought or irritation that you find annoying.

3. In the right column list arguments counter to your annoyances.

4. Consider the following in creating your counter arguments:

    a. Perspective: How important is the annoying behavior to you in the "big picture"?

    b. Harm to yourself: What is the actual harm that the annoying behavior is doing directly to you?

    c. Irritation to others: How might your irritation be affecting people around you?

    d. Under your control or not: What actual control do you have over this annoying behavior? If you have some indirect influence, ask yourself if you are taking that action. If not, consider accepting the annoying behavior as "part of life."

Failure to Forgive: It's not worth it

FOR MANY PEOPLE, a major obstacle in finding happiness is harboring grudges and failing to forgive.

A number of years ago I met a woman whose philandering husband had left her virtually penniless at his untimely death. Although her husband had died two years earlier, she was still seething, unable to get past her anger. Unhappy during most of her marriage, she continued in a state of misery, her husband still controlling her life.

To blame is to lose control. While blame may be understandable, it centers all your energy on the negative. Just as importantly, it places control of your emotions in the hands of the blamed individual, beyond your reach. Nelson Mandela, who was imprisoned for 27 years, was once asked how he was able to bring himself to forgive his jailers. His reply was humanity at its best:

> "When I walked out of the gate I knew that if I continued to hate these people I was still in prison."

Unlike the widow above, he moved on, not controlled by hate or blame.

Some actions are so awful that they cry out for blame. But people who are able to overcome blame avoid narrowing their lives. While blame restricts, forgiveness frees. Where blame interferes with constructive problem solving, forgiveness opens life to new possibilities.

Most people incorrectly believe that forgiveness means accepting the guilty person's actions and absolving them of responsibility. On the contrary, you may still find the actions detestable, but forgiving them allows you to move forward rather than replaying past wrongs. Long term anger and resentment serve only to hurt *you*, both emotionally and physically. Forgiveness is for *you*. It allows you to increase control of your life.

It may take repeated tries, but remember, navigating the path to happiness means walking over some uncomfortable stones.

Exercise

Getting Over a Big Boulder: Forgiveness

1. State the offending behavior.

2. List — and writing is critical — all the circumstances that may have influenced the guilty party's actions. For example, "He had a miserable childhood himself."

   a.

   b.

   c.

3. Write down what not forgiving does to you. How has it harmed you already and how may it harm your future?

   a.

   b.

   c.

Overview of Section 2

Attend to Your Perceptions

WE HUMANS ARE extraordinary receptacles, receiving millions of messages everyday — auditory, visual, tactile, smell, and taste. Every second we receive so much stimulation that a room full of scientists could hardly monitor it all. It's like a cake mix with a million ingredients constantly changing. Somehow the merged input produces what we perceive as life.

These perceptions, in turn, determine how we feel and function. They determine our state of happiness or sadness. Shakespeare had it right, when he wrote, *"It is not in the stars to hold our destiny but in ourselves."* It is the perceptions of the massive daily input of information that guide our thoughts, which, in turn, dictate our feelings and subsequently our behavior.

Perceptions, influenced by our biology but mostly learned, are the way we organize information. Attitudes, biases, moods, fall under this concept.

Understanding our general mental tendencies, or our perceptions, goes a long way into comprehending how we deal with the world. If we are basically pessimistic, that will not tell us how we might act in every situation, but it will give us a big step up in revealing how we are likely to act a significant portion of the time. Whether we come from a position of fear, inadequacy, worry, optimism, confidence or assertiveness clarifies a great deal about our thoughts, feelings and behavior. When we further define these perceptions into tendencies in specific situations such as social gatherings, work setting, and family meetings, we increase our understanding of the individual.

Knowledge of our perceptions can help others understand us, but more importantly, self-knowledge of our perceptions can be decisive in directing our own thinking, emotions and behavior. Take someone who tends to anticipate the worst. Almost by definition such a perspective will lead to significant anxiety and avoidance of the unfamiliar. In contrast a confident person might relish new experiences.

Awareness of our own perceptions tells us where we presently are. It does not tell where we can go. The unassertive can become assertive, the shy more outgoing, pessimists more optimistic and so forth. If we can clarify our perceptions and thinking we can redirect our lives to be happier and more fruitful.

CHAPTER 9

What Kind Of Glasses Do You Wear?

PSYCHOTHERAPY OFTEN REQUIRES clients to change the kind of glasses they wear. Not literally, of course, but as a metaphor for changing the way we "take in" in the world. Psychologists may call this "reframing" the problem but, whatever the descriptor, a new way of looking at an old issue is involved.

Changing your outlook is not easy. There are reasons we maintain the patterns we do. Most often the underlying reason is a belief, a benefit or a fear. Here are some simple examples where new glasses need to be prescribed. A client is working 90 hours a week and has over-committed on top of that. He is not enjoying life, feels overly stressed and has a number of generalized physical pains. His doctor says he's killing himself working such outlandish hours, but he has a well-entrenched belief that he must work hard for the betterment of his family.

In therapy he reveals high perfectionist standards, beliefs that were developed in his upbringing by a very strict, demanding and critical father. Although that may be the origin of his personal standards, it is his current thinking patterns that are likely to be the focus of therapeutic attention — that is, his particular kind of glasses. His present glasses provide the view, "My wife won't love me unless I give her a beautiful home. I'm not a success unless I'm perfect, the way my father expected me to be. I can only succeed if I work harder than everyone else." Changing those glasses to allow for more imperfections, self-compassion and a mature identity would be a major but achievable goal.

His underlying fear of failure and his insatiable drive to succeed are camouflaged by a rationale concerning the betterment of his family. While his emotions are real, his personal sense of worthiness is based on satisfying his father's standards, not his own, and possibly not those of his wife. Changing the lenses through which he views reality would likely alter his behavior and his life.

Another common example involves glasses that deflect the positive and absorb the negative. This pattern is evident in those with poor self-esteem who focus on their deficits while underplaying their attributes. Such individuals are virtually always capable, but their inability to acknowledge their positive qualities and to see only their perceived deficits is the real problem, not their lack of talent. Their glasses filter reality in a way that guarantees continued feelings of inadequacy.

Other people permit a problem, be it a relationship or a temporary setback, to dominate their perspective. They allow themselves to become victims of circumstances. They forget previous life challenges they've overcome and become paralyzed by the problem at hand, overlooking the skills used in previous difficulties. Their emotional upset has fogged their lenses.

Still others believe that bad luck or people outside their control are dictating their lives. Their view underplays the portion of their problem that they can control and gives too much power to others. In each case, it is the perception through their glasses that is at the core of the difficulty.

Of course, problematic relatives, accidents and unhappy events can cause difficulties, but it is not the external issues alone that create our despair. It is how we view and manage these challenges.

When you're angry, anxious, depressed or upset, you might want to check your glasses. Maybe it's time to change your prescription. You may see better on your path to happiness.

Exercise

Wear the Right Glasses on Your Path

Examine the manner in which you are looking at a particularly challenging problem and consider whether your "glasses" are obstructing your options.

A. Write down some of your dominant perceptual styles of approaching the world. For example, do you believe that you are confident or insecure, assertive or unassertive, pessimistic or optimistic, blameful or personally responsible, etc? Write them out.

B. Write down a long-standing or pressing problem. For example: unemployment, time stresses, financial issues, loneliness, etc.

C. How do your glasses – the perceptual style you identified in "A" — influence how you approach your long-standing or pressing issue?

D. If your glasses play a significant role in dealing with your problem, you might want to consider modifying your approach. For example, you may consider that your issue is caused by outside factors without examining what you can control and working on that. In this example consider again what you can do to manage your emotions regardless of the outside factors.

E. Write out your new perception of what you can do to make lessen your problem or your reaction to it.

CHAPTER 10

Our Internal Dialog

No MATTER HOW intimate our relationships with others, we ultimately reside in a cocoon shared by no one else. Inside that vessel we think continuously and thereby create our moods, attitudes and expectations. So it is not a stretch to say that if we want to gain greater control of our well being, we need turn no further than our internal chatter.

In everyday life, our interpretations of reality make us vulnerable to unhappiness. In our self-talk we over generalize, blame others for our problems, focus on the negative and berate ourselves with "shoulds" and "musts" — to mention a few of the most common unhealthy mental habits. Let me expand on each of these.

Over-generalizing simply means that we take one event and expand it beyond reasonable assumptions. It is a common pattern of those who are anxious, worried, or depressed. "I've lost my job. I'm a failure." "I'm divorced, nobody will ever love me." These may seem obvious misperceptions to others, but not to the person thinking them. An event happens and we over generalize. We create an inappropriate label, a worry or fear. Recall some of your deepest anxieties, and you'll likely remember distortions that you believed at the time. The deeper the fear, the more likely the overgeneralization. However, as Mark Twain remarked, "Ninety-eight percent of what I worried about never happened."

Blaming others may seem an obvious fault when observed in others but not so easily recognized when we are guilty of it. Blaming others for our distress means that we inadvertently give up power. If that incorrigible relative gets under our skin and ruins our day, it is he or she who has the power over our emotions, not ourselves. While it may be true that the relative's behavior is uncouth, despicable, and inconsiderate, your anger is unlikely to alter their behavior and may even facilitate it. Attending to what you can control in the circumstance is virtually always the best strategy.

"I'm a lazy sloth" may be an overgeneralization but it is also an example of focusing on the negative. My common response to such statements is, "OK, prove it. Keep a diary of your activity, hour by hour, and let's see whether you really are a sloth." The most common outcome is that, although the individual may be less productive than he would like, he is hardly a sloth. He has focused on the negative, not seeing the positive. When a more evenhanded perception is established, the problem-solving process can begin. Perceiving oneself as a sloth gets you nowhere. When you find yourself focusing exclusively on the negative, it's time to seek a more balanced view.

Another common mental distortion is the over use of the words, "should" and "must," as in "I should never make a mistake" or "I must have a perfectly clean house." While no one likes to make mistakes, and a clean house is an admirable goal, the use of these words in the extreme cause untold mental anguish. Many confuse personal *likes* with "shoulds" and "musts". It would be nice if everyone liked me but unreasonable to expect it. And while it is nice to have a clean house, it is destructive to obsess about it. It would be wonderful if our children never encountered problems, but it's decidedly unlikely. It would be nice if others viewed our opinions as always right, but silly to expect so. To expect otherwise, taking the path of "shoulds" and "musts", leads to emotional distress.

There is truth in the claim that happiness is an attitude or a state of mind. Likewise much of our unhappiness is of our own making — starting with our internal conversation. However, changing thought patterns is not as easy as it appears. We have well-rehearsed reasons for exaggerating our fears, blaming others, focusing on the negative and abiding by our "shoulds" and "musts." Nevertheless, in seeking greater happiness, awareness of these mental distortions is a good place to start. Mental distortions tend to get us off of the path to happiness.

Exercise
Attend to Your Internal Dialog as You Travel

It may appear obvious that our thinking is the basis for our moods. Nevertheless, most of us fail to accept how close that link is and recognize that altering our thinking is the most direct manner to take control of our mood. To begin to understand the strength of the relationship between your thinking and your mood, keep a diary of thoughts and emotions for the next five days.

Record those daily moments during which you are feeling most distressed, note the intensity from 1 to 10 (10 being the most distressed) and briefly write out your most prominent thoughts.

Day	Mood State	Mood 1-10	Thoughts
1			
2			
3			
4			
5			

———— ✻ ————

CHAPTER 11

You Can Handle More Than You Realize

I COMPLIMENTED A friend yesterday on how well she is handling a life threatening illness. Her reply is well worth remembering.

She downplayed her own admirable management of a serious health issue for the last two years and quickly identified a mutual friend who was dealing with something even more severe. In doing so, she reminded me that those who cope well express empathy for others who are in an even more challenging place.

Those who wallow in "Why did this happen to me?" or a "This is so unfair" mentality have a steep mountain to climb. My friend stays away from that trap. Instead, she compares her problems with someone less well off. In doing so she puts her problem in perspective and implicitly expresses gratitude that her situation isn't any worse than it is.

She also turned the table and complimented me on my handling of a lifetime issue. I realized that, while I questioned my own ability to manage her serious problem, she, in turn, wondered if she could manage mine. How typical of her and, I think, of many of us. When we think of facing serious challenges such as dealing with the loss of a loved one, a life-threatening illness, or a sudden disability, we are terrified. In the abstract we often believe that we are totally incapable of surviving such tragedies. And yet in reality, overwhelmingly, we do.

If you were a clinical psychologist 30 years ago, your focus on a new patient would undoubtedly be exclusively on their problems.

Your training would have taught you to look for patterns, family history and factors that influenced their concerns. What would be absent, or at least underemphasized, in your analysis would be the patient's strengths. That omission is significant. Modern clinicians don't overlook the strengths that each of us brings to a crisis.

Many of us make the mistake of forgetting that we have a repertoire of mental health coping skills that need to be unearthed when a crisis arises. The problem stems from the fact that we bury certain fears, like the potential loss of a loved one, so deeply that we forget our strengths as well. There is much to be said for living in the present. But not if, in stifling our fears, we fail to remember that we have managed pain before and are capable of handling it again.

If you were to survey 20 people regarding the tragedies suffered during their lives, you would amass an astonishing list: abandonment, physical and psychological abuse, divorce, family alcoholism, and deaths of close relatives and friends. The list would go on and on. Most of these situations leave scars of varying degrees. Yet people survive and learn. The resilience of humans is remarkable. Our survival skills emerge and are mostly enhanced by living through life's trials.

My recommendation is not to obsess over potential disasters. But do recognize that you bring strengths to problems that you will confront. You have already faced extraordinary difficulties and have survived. Some may have taken time to overcome, but you have. Recognize what you've already been through and have confidence that you can manage future challenges. It may not be easy, but with those skills in hand you'll manage again when the time comes.

Exercise

Remember Your Strengths as You Travel

If you could trade lives with anyone who would you be? Don't just pick their good qualities or fame or wealth, but the whole package, good and bad. It's interesting to contemplate because when we dig deep into virtually everyone's life we find challenges beneath the surface. The examination reveals that we all have had to face tragedies, and most found the inner strength to survive the obstacles. Unfortunately, during new difficulties, we are prone to forget the personal strength that carried us over the obstacles in the past and can again. We forget those skills are still within our repertoire.

Write down the two most difficult problems you have faced in your life.

1.
2.

Write down the personal characteristics that helped you get through the above challenges.

1.
2.
3.

Write down which of your inner strengths are likely to come to fore in the future.

1.
2.
3.

CHAPTER 12

My Father Died

You CAN'T TELL someone's feelings by just knowing his or her outward circumstances. Oh, there might be some relationship between happy surroundings and feeling good or very difficult surroundings and feeling sad — but the correlation is low. A prime example of this surfaced when a patient of mine was absolutely euphoric after his beloved father died.

I had been seeing Howard for about two months and making little progress. It was obvious that he was severely depressed and his medications were not making much difference. He expressed most of the classical signs of depression: poor sleep, loss of appetite, low energy, some cognitive impairment, irritability, lack of concentration, and feelings of hopelessness and helplessness. Particularly challenging for our interactions was his unwillingness to discuss what was bothering him. His one saving grace was his interest in continuing to meet every week, always arriving on time and seemingly pleased to be there.

So I was surprised when Howard unexpectedly missed two weeks running. Even more amazing was his demeanor when he showed up — alive and energetic. Still more shocking was Howard's reply to my inquiry as to what had happened to him. "My father died," was his reply.

Ordinarily such a reply would, of course, elicit an expression of sympathy for the grieving that one assumed was present. But Howard wasn't grieving. He was happy, happier than he had been for years. It seems that his earlier depression stemmed in large part from an estrangement from his father, his only living relative. The conflict that caused the estrangement had occurred over a decade earlier for reasons that Howard didn't fully understand, but that he felt were intractable and could be his fault. He claimed to have attempted to reconcile with his father on many occasions only to be sternly rebuffed, and ultimately he had lost all hope of ever seeing his father again.

Shortly after his previous visit to the clinic, Howard received a call from a local hospital that his father was there, dying, and wanted to see him. What he found when he arrived was a frail man filled with contrition and sorrow. With the two of them falling over one another in apologies and regrets, they then settled down to reminisce about good times together. This went on for over a week, until Howard's father succumbed to his illness. In the process, Howard lost the tremendous guilt that had racked his mind and left him feeling hopeless. He no longer shouldered the full responsibility for the issues that separated him and his father and even came to recognize that his assumptions concerning how his father perceived him were wrong. New memories replaced old distorted ones and left him with a positive feeling of closure.

Anyone seeing Howard after his father died would not see a depressed man — the stooping shoulders and lethargy were gone. But to fully appreciate the transition from depression to euphoria, it is important to recognize that we humans are not stimulus-response beings. "The mind is its own place and in itself, can make a heaven of hell, a hell of heaven," said John Milton in one of my favorite quotes. It refers to the fact that our feelings are not directly a function of circumstance. How we *process* the situation determines our emotional experience and the subsequent feelings and behavior that follow. Between the inputs we receive and our feelings is our interpretation of events. It is there where we make our interpretations that determine how we function, and ultimately our happiness.

For those many years before his father's death Howard chose to blame himself, based upon partial information as well as his own distortions. The guilt that engulfed him and subsequently caused a deep depression is not something Howard would say he intentionally chose, but he did, in the fashion that our mind and habits are ultimately responsible for the perceptions we experience.

It doesn't feel like a choice because it seems so automatic but it is a choice. Abraham Lincoln had it right, "Most people are about as happy as they make up their minds to be."

Exercise

Your Path May Take New Turns

Recall a negative belief that has plagued you throughout your life. Write it out below.

Challenge the accuracy of the above belief remembering to be very specific in your description, very balanced and fair (considering such things as your age and circumstances) and as objective as you can be. Give your belief a sense of perspective. Lastly, be kind to yourself.

Rewrite your belief below with the above considerations in mind.

CHAPTER 13

Half a Man or More Than Whole?

WE'VE ALL HAD experiences that become locked in our minds forever. One such event happened to me during my years working in a rehabilitation hospital. The hospital in question had been built at the turn of the 20th century and its long, long hallways reeked of age, despair and loss.[9]

Into this scene came a man who physically was only half a man, existing only from the waist up, and who was seen virtually all the time on his moving platform. My half man — and interestingly I can't remember his name — navigated around the long hallways by lying on his stomach and propelling his flatbed vehicle with his hands in the manner that a child pushes a scooter.

Beyond the shock of a man coming toward you on a low gurney was what followed — a big smile, an exuberant greeting. No introvert he, but an embrace of you, the day –- life! It took a few minutes to adjust to hearing this upbeat voice from below, a greeting from an unexpected angle and a physical presence never before encountered. I have no idea of his inner life but, judging from his outer attitude, I'd say his mental health was extraordinarily positive — especially in light of the challenges he faced.

How does a person accept that he has half a body? Functionally, the same way any of us accepts our failings. It only appears different

---

9 Drake Rehabilitation Hospital, a division of the University of Cincinnati College of Medicine. It has been since modernized.

because of its magnitude and extreme rarity. It may seem beyond our imagination, but in the private domain of our minds, we, like him, must sustain our sense of self and ward off our fears. We must manage our inadequacies, whether real or perceived, so they don't overwhelm us. We must focus and be grateful for what we have.

So, is it realistic, to compare a man with such profound physical challenges to the issues that we face on a daily basis: a lost wallet, a crashed computer, a social slight, a bent fender, a bad cold? I believe it is. Each of us gets up each day dealing with a myriad of challenges, coping strategies and attitudes. I can only assume that the man navigating the rehab hospital had favorite people, meals, goals, memories, and anticipations. I expect that he had to manage fears, anxieties, potential depression and insults. In that sense he is no different than any of us. When we focus on his extreme disability, it is easy to see the differences and be blind to the similarities. Still, whether able-bodied, wealthy or poor, no matter our racial or ethnic make-up, we must all handle the challenges of life.

The vision of a well functioning half man can evoke inspiration, awe. It motivates us to be grateful for what we have — temporarily. I say temporarily because, as incredible as such a story is, we can't sustain the perspective unless we take a lesson from it. The lessons I take are often invoked in these chapters: acceptance of who we are and focus on control of what we can control. If you've read this far, you've seen these messages time and time again, because they are central to well being and easily slip away during periods of crisis or stress.

Acceptance of who we are focuses on our makeup — a complex of marvelous values, attributes and talents combined with human failings. So, by all means, stand in awe that someone with so obvious a challenge as a man with half a body can greet others in a buoyant fashion. Then look beyond the outer being and imagine his inner life and what we can learn. It's that inner life that, to me, is the most illuminating.

CHAPTER 14

Everyone Should Live a Year in Winnipeg

"Nine months of winter and three months of sloppy skating" is a common adage among residents of Winnipeg, Manitoba, Canada. I know because in my twenties I lived there for three years. I found that this description is not actually true because, while the brutal winter does seem to last forever, the short summers can be uncomfortably hot, providing something to gripe about year round, if you're so inclined. Let me quickly add that I loved the people and the culture, if not the weather.

In spite of the weather, or perhaps partly because of it, I look back on those years with fondness, because I learned a lot about myself. How you survive a difficult time tells you much. I believe there are two aspects — how you manage the challenge and what lessons you take from the experience.

In my case the time in Winnipeg was a period of learning and growing. I was a new university teacher and, if truth be told, not a very good one yet. But I was steadfast and able to get my bearings. I closely watched those around me who were successful and attempted to model their behavior. For the first time I realized that success was based more on relationships than knowledge, assuming a reasonable baseline. My focus was more on these relationships than the harsh weather.

But permanent residents of Winnipeg seemed quite happy in spite of the weather. You may find it interesting to note that those countries with bleak climates actually have happier populations on the whole than counties closer to the equator. It's not a perfect correlation, but it's generally true. I know, it's contrary to intuition, but the data is consistent.

Early experiences often become anchors, a term used in psychology to mean a standard by which we compare. Since that time, I have used Winnipeg's weather as my anchor and in that light almost all weather is absolutely wonderful.

Struggling through adversity is an opportunity to raise your level of gratefulness. When I begin to grouse about inclement weather, I recall how much more extreme and uncomfortable it was in Winnipeg. This mental exercise reduces frustration and heightens gratefulness. Both are aids to happiness and well being, and there is a lesson here beyond this simple example of a harsh climate.

I know of no one who hasn't suffered adversities — death of a loved one, a bad relationship, divorce, loneliness, addiction, poverty, severe illness or disability. Virtually all of us have experienced at least one of these hardships. The question is what did we learn from these trials. Instead of merely hiding them in a box, I believe it is wise to reframe them to our advantage. The fact that you survived is itself worth noting. It's also likely that you dug down to inner strengths that you may not have been aware of at the time. Recall those strengths such as perseverance, creativity, hard work, methodical planning.

Think about how you grew from the experience. Remember the doubts and fears you experienced. Notice that they may have been much worse than your current ones, yet you got through them.

When you have an anchor to recall, like the weather in Winnipeg, things can look quite sunny.

CHAPTER 15

The Pleasures of Aging

OF COURSE EVERYONE wants to live a long life when given the alternative. But few consider the positive nature of becoming "mature." In our youth-oriented society the old are often considered washed up, depleted and inferior. The young, with their beauty and vigor, seem an obvious preference.

But there are marvelous advantages to getting old — things to look forward to. Developments that cause most older people to say, "This is the happiest time of my life. There is no way I would trade this time for my youth."

Without a doubt there are burdens that come with the years, such as aches, pains and more limited movement, but even with these encumbrances, maturity has its advantages.

A story I was told many years ago illustrates some of the most important. Two men were talking about their childhoods when one mentioned that he was born very late in his parents' lives. When he was in his early teens, his father was in his mid-sixties. "Good grief," the other exclaimed. "You missed the whole father bonding experience. You never got to play catch with your dad." "On the contrary," the other man replied, "I got to really spend time with my dad. He was retired. He no longer felt the stress of his job and had time to spend with me. We walked, he listened, talked and he was really there when I needed him."

Most older people are less tense and worried than the young. The quest to conquer the world has passed. Their spark isn't necessarily gone, but it's not as urgent as it used be. There is less to prove. Accomplishments tend not to be so tied up with ego. Not true for every retired person, but true for most.

There are other characteristic patterns found with passing years. Many contribute to the greater sense of happiness that social scientists have repeatedly documented in older people.

Reflect for a second on the following words: wisdom, patience, perspective, knowledge, understanding, worldliness and thoughtfulness. Quickly judge whether you're more likely to assign each word to the young or the old. Not a perfect correlation, but I would wager most of these fine characteristics would land in the older category more often than the younger one.

Or take the following aphorisms: "Don't sweat the small stuff," "This too will pass." Again, the same quiz. Quick, no consideration — just your immediate reaction. Place it in the young or old category? If you're like me, these philosophies are much more likely to be placed in the older pile.

In particular maturity nurtures perspective. The experiences of life provide lessons, lessons not yet learned by the young. Older people have endured more trials and tribulations and they have survived. They know the difference between inconveniences and catastrophes. They know about failure, sickness, sorrow, loss and grief. They're not fun but the older have gotten through them and will again. They've seen a lot and it's not quite so frightening.

Another heightened characteristic is gratitude, a pillar of the happiness formula. Many older people appear to excel in it. Perhaps they know that the end of their lives is nearer and this increases their appreciation of the pleasures they have. Perhaps a greater incidence of friends and relatives experiencing physical problems makes their own troubles less significant and helps them appreciate what they have. Maybe it's just an increased sensitivity to small favors because the big pursuits are behind them. Whatever the cause, older people tend to pause and count their good fortune more often.

Friendships, too, often take on added value. Time with friends is chosen, not obligatory. The responsibilities of children are fewer. The pleasures of grandparenting are far more pleasurable for most than the full weight of raising children.

Yes, for these and a multitude of other privileges, most older people do not wish to trade their lot for youth.

CHAPTER 16

The Joys of Pain

I DO NOT want to go to heaven if heaven is a place without pain. I do not want to go to an afterlife if such a place is without suffering. I wish to grieve, be sad and even have temporary bouts of depression. No, I am not crazy, deranged or "off my rocker." I simply believe that an occasional measure of pain and suffering is better than total bliss.

Such bliss would reek of psychosis if it were not sprinkled with the setbacks that make life real. Pain and suffering are the ingredients of life that make joy, laughter and even happiness possible. My recipe calls for a full spoonful of pepper, a flourish of vinegar, and a dash of lime, things that cause a life to be sharp, bitter and tart. I have no recipes devoid of seasoning. A daily diet of vanilla is, for me, a pain I wish to totally avoid.

Undoubtedly there are those who complain their diet is overwrought with spice. Where there should be a dash there is a flow, where there should be a pinch there is a stream. To be sure, too much of a good thing can be bad and too much of a bad thing can be worse. But my complaint is against those who miss the value of pain, who see no worth in suffering, who somehow act as if they should be privileged beyond others. I am critical of those who bemoan daily irritations as if life should be without inconvenience. I see them as whiny, self-centered and bereft of perspective. I fault their inability to understand the difference between a problem and an inconvenience. When you have no food, shelter and no prospects of either, you have a problem. Everything else is an inconvenience.

Without inconvenience life would be boring. Sameness and dullness would rule the day. Laughter would have no counterpoint and provide no relief if it were not for life's inconveniences. And what would life be without laughter?

Joy, too, could hardly be appreciated without frustration. Tear streaked moments of joy come about after mountains have been climbed, rivers crossed, and fears faced, each with its own heart throbbing anxiety. The lives of those who have been given privilege and wealth, those for whom most of life's everyday inconveniences have been removed, are often spent searching for purpose in order to gain a sense of self. They seem to sense that a life without work, devoid of a struggle, is empty. Personal identity emerges from the struggles, the pain, and the battles we each face. Each effort carries with it the frustrations of life, the inconveniences. To reach the mountain top simply by being placed there offers little sense of accomplishment and feels barren compared to those who have struggled to reach a lofty place.

Suffering, too, has its place. In its presence I have felt my strongest kinship. It is where I have come closest to a sense of dignity, even a feeling of grandeur. Suffering offers the greatest challenge, the greatest test. I definitely do not wish to live a life of suffering for that, too, would rob me of those other exquisite emotions I treasure. But to have a life without suffering would lessen the intensity of my joys, laughter and sensitivity to others who are experiencing their own suffering. Our songs and books would soon grow dull.

Go to your blissful heaven if you must. Imagine that place without pain, suffering, and inconvenience. Ahh, not to be bothered, irritated, annoyed forever and ever and ever and ever. A place without tears, with little drama, no sorrow, no regrets. No accomplishments either, for what's an accomplishment without an obstacle? How would you differ from others? No mind, you would be blissful. It is neither a bliss I can imagine nor one that I seek.

A Tibetan prayer

Grant that I may be given appropriate difficulties and suffering on this journey so that my heart may be truly awakened and my practice of liberation and universal compassion may be truly fulfilled.

CHAPTER 17

Not All Things Long Ago Were Wonderful

I RECENTLY FINISHED teaching a class entitled, *The Male Experience: Past and Present.* I've taught it about eight times and it's one of my favorites. The nature of masculinity in America has changed so dramatically during the last century that it boggles the mind.

If you were a boy born 100 or 150 years ago, you would likely have grown up in a home where fathers barely had contact with their children and even more rarely expressed any warmth toward them. The adage that children were to be seen and not heard was a practiced principle, children viewed by party guests and then dismissed. Contrast that picture with the common sight today of a father pushing a stroller — or a baby carriage, as they used to be called — or walking hand in hand with a toddler. Unimaginable just a few generations back. The contrast between the two parenting styles is striking.

It's important to clearly state that a poor upbringing does not dictate personal destiny. Many a child reared by emotionally distant parents grow into a mature adult. However, poor home experiences do create an obstacle to overcome. A cold parenting style, in particular, appears to impair a child's ability to understand, interpret and understand the emotions of others. The ability to "read" another's emotions is at the heart of what psychologists call emotional intelligence — a strength that is invaluable in forming intimate relationships.

The importance of forming close relationships, a central ingredient of happiness, is illustrated in the results of a study that began in 1938 and followed 238 students for life. The students were tested and interviewed every few years for the remainder of their lives, continuing to this day. Study director, Harvard psychology professor, George Valliant, recently reported a critical finding. Of the 31 men in the study who were *incapable* of forming intimate relationships, only 13% are still alive. Of those who were better at forming relationships, more than one-third still lives. His study confirms that having even one intimate relationship can lessen the challenges of life and strongly contribute to living longer.[10]

Among the many consistent findings in the well being research literature is the understanding that strong relationships breed happiness. There is, of course, much to fret about in our society. But it is important for our well being to recognize that, within our lifetime, there has been social progress unimaginable a century ago. In my opinion, the extraordinary evolution from an emotionally distant dad to one who clearly expresses his warmth and caring is a change to recognize and celebrate. So the next time you see that father toting his infant on his shoulders, reading a story to his child or pushing a carriage, give yourself an emotional lift by mentally noting that yes, indeed, some marvelous changes have occurred and are occurring. Much better to be alert to the good things than wallow in the negative.

---

10 Vaillant, G. and Mukamal, K., *Successful Aging*, The American Journal of Psychiatry, Volume 158, Issue 6, June 2001, pp. 839-847.

CHAPTER 18

Happiness By Another Measure

WE LIVE MANY lives. Progressing through stages of childhood, adolescence and chapters of adulthood, we experience changes in our behaviors, attitudes and philosophies. Changes that amaze when reflected upon.

I love to listen to people's life stories, always intrigued by the many turns most of us take. I often rhetorically ask, "Could you ever believe that you would travel such a path?" "Never in a million years," most say.

I'd have to say the same inquiry applies to happiness. In your youth, what did you think would lead you down the yellow brick road? Here again, the answers reflect astonishment over how life has turned out.

Interestingly, many of the happier lives we lived were not replete with material goods, fame or acknowledgement. Often they were struggling times, periods where goals and purpose were primary. Happiness doesn't seem to correlate with vast material wealth and power.

A recent newspaper account of Abd Al-Rahman III, an emir and caliph of Cordoba in 10th century Spain, illustrates this point. This absolute ruler had virtually everything young people of today often yearn for — fame, wealth and a variety of sexual partners. As a powerful ruler he could demand any of these things from his dominions and more. And yet, toward the end of his life, he is quoted as saying,

"I have now reigned above 50 years in victory or peace; beloved by my subjects, dreaded by my enemies, and respected by my allies. Riches and honors, power and pleasure, have waited on my call, nor does any earthly blessing appear to have been wanting to my felicity." However, he goes on to say, "I have diligently numbered the days of pure and genuine happiness which have fallen to my lot. They amount to 14."

One's man's observations are seldom universally true, but Abd Al-Rahman III's musings do raise an interesting question. Are the things we seek the real path to happiness?

Conservative New York Times' columnist David Brooks recently presented a modern day version of this question. Long known for his political observations and societal insights, Mr. Brooks frequently comments on his personal introspection. His latest book, *The Road to Character*, is one such example. In spite of lofty accomplishments, he finds his life somewhat wanting and wrestles with personal questions of identity and purpose. He notes, "I'm paid to be a narcissistic blowhard" and at another point, "I was born with a natural disposition toward shallowness." These self-deprecations are meant to illustrate his *uncertainty* that his highly lauded achievements are enough to equate with a fulfilled life. Instead, he evokes historical figures who examined their personal weaknesses and sought to compensate by working for others. These are the people Brooks says he would like to emulate.[11]

Mr. Brooks notes that there are two sets of virtues, resume and eulogy virtues. He notes that while the resume virtues list accomplishments touted in the workplace, it is the eulogy virtues — like being loving and generous or having integrity and perseverance that are mentioned at your funeral. Something to think about.

---

11 For example, author Brooks, describes the many contributions of Franklin Delano Roosevelt's cabinet, none of whom felt it necessary to write their memoirs –- an action Mr. Brooks says is often self-aggrandizing.

Exercise
The Best Measure as You Travel Your Path to Happiness

Think about your life not as what you have accomplished in a professional sense but who you are as a person — what personal characteristics you are most proud of.

Write down those characteristics that you would like others to describe at your funeral or life's testimonial.

1.

2.

3.

4.

5.

CHAPTER 19

Pain and Happiness: Two sides of the same coin

My professional career has been two-sided in the sense that the first half was spent treating those with pain and suffering, and the second half has focused on happiness. While not immediately apparent, these two fields are surprisingly intertwined.

Perhaps the most striking similarity between pain and happiness is that they are both perceptions. They each may begin as an external incident, a hurtful action for pain, a loving compliment for happiness, but the brain must process each external event. And what is happening in the brain in the form of attitude, expectation, beliefs, etc., plays a significant role in our actual experience, be it pain or happiness. Thus, one man's pain is another man's pleasure and vice versa. Our *interpretation* of what is happening externally is at the crux of whether we are generally happy or miserable.

Now, some may rush to say that physical and psychological pain are strikingly different. In actuality the differences are far less than most realize. Studies show that an intense psychological hurt, such as the loss of a loved one, stimulate the same areas of the brain as does intense physical pain. If anything, my observations are that psychological distress is more troublesome than physical pain. Many a child would rather endure a quick spanking than the disapproval of a loving parent.

All this is to say that it is necessary when considering happiness to not only study habits of kindness, gratitude, exercise, etc. — the positive practices of well being — but also to study how we handle pain, especially psychological pain.

Let me give one example. The world famous theoretical physicist, Stephen Hawking, was diagnosed in his early 20's with a motor neuron disease that left him trapped in a shell of a body. Now 63, he is unable to move any part of his body, is confined to a wheelchair and speaks through a mechanical voice instrument. An interviewer asked what kept his spirits up. He replied, "My expectations were reduced to zero when I was 21. Everything since then has been a bonus."

It is that interpretation, a philosophical adjustment, that is at the heart of what we all, perhaps to a much lesser degree, must make to the painful experiences of life. Hawking made an extraordinarily positive adjustment. How we respond to the challenges of life determines our life's emotional trajectory.

Consider — if you were presented with the choice between a life with chronic pain but continued speech and mobility versus the neurological shell of a body experienced by Stephen Hawking, what alternative would you take? As difficult as the former might be, the latter incarceration into the body of a Stephen Hawking and the accompanying psychological adjustment might tip you away from that alternative. And so it is likely that you would choose the alternative of chronic pain versus, in my mind, the more emotionally challenging experience of a completely paralyzed body. The fact that some of you would choose otherwise is again evidence that our pain and happiness are not absolutes, but shaped by our individual attitudes and values.

My purpose is not to create uncomfortable scenarios, but rather to emphasize that we all face challenges in life. If we choose to believe that we are helpless victims, we are likely to be unhappy. On the other hand, if we control what we can manage in the face of our various losses and hurts, we are more likely to maximize our well being.

You may wish to live a life without pain. But, even if such a wish could be granted, consider that your happiness is more pronounced when contrasted with sadness. Sunshine is better after rain. Health is valued more after illness. And love is, indeed, more intense after its absence. But, of course, we want mostly sunshine, mostly health and our loved ones to be with us most, but definitely not all, of the time.

So it is true that we prefer mostly happiness. But that happiness is also dependent upon how we handle the inevitable experiences of pain. To live life to its fullest we must not only practice happiness habits, but manage the degree to which pain, psychological and physical, controls us.

CHAPTER 20

Frustrations

In David Eagleman's fanciful book, *Sum: Tales of the Afterlife*, the reader relives all life experiences reshuffled and grouped together. For example, we might have six months of sex, sleep for 30 years, spend six days cutting our nails, two months driving in front of our house, two and a half years standing in line at the Bureau of Motor Vehicles, as well as 15 months looking for things we've lost. It's fun to look at the pleasures, but grouping the frustrations together — whoa, that's rough!

Both frustrations and pleasures typically don't come all at once, but bunches can occur and, when we've had a "bad" day or week, frustrations certainly seem to occur unfairly.

Recently I drove my car to the dealership for a simple repair, having been assured that the ordered part was on hand. Upon arrival I learned that there had been a miscommunication between departments and, no, the car couldn't be repaired that morning. Later that week our car broke down at the beginning of a long trip, causing delays and alterations in our plans. In the big realm of things, not the end of the world, but imagine living through these inconveniences for months at a time.

Managing frustration is tough. What do we do with bumps in our life? Of course, we can throw a fit or have an outburst about other people's incompetence. We can stew, allowing ourselves to focus on bad luck.

Some people allow frustration to linger longer than necessary. They blame others, which puts the responsibility for change outside of their control. Take the example of getting stuck in traffic. Of course, traffic jams are irritating and we can't control how long they last, but ultimately, how long we stay frustrated is up to each of us. When we smolder, we are often guilty of thinking that "these things shouldn't happen" or are "always happening to me"— tendencies that make the blood boil hotter and longer.

People who manage frustrations well think differently. They're more likely to think; "It's not going on my permanent record. Tomorrow is another day. It's not a problem, it's an inconvenience. It is what it is." These are thoughts that put daily frustrations into perspective. Perspective lessens the impact of frustration and encourages movement to other distractions and healthy behaviors.

So does balance. While frustrations are annoying, reminders of the positive experiences in life offset frustration's power to bring us down. Most of us are incredibly fortunate to live the lives we do with all of the relationships and amenities we enjoy. To allow inconveniences to dominate those advantages for more than a short time is a personal failing that we can rectify. Reminding ourselves of the good things in our lives on a regular basis helps to do just that.

Those who handle frustrations well also tend *not* to generalize or exaggerate. They stay factual. Traffic jams happen. Cars break down. Technology fails. Frustrating problems are difficult enough. No need to magnify the challenge beyond the issue at hand.

It's true that lousy things happen, and sometimes even in bunches. Although it may feel differently at times, there is no exterior force that has picked us out to create havoc in our life. To believe otherwise is to give in to superstition and paranoia. If we learn to handle the everyday annoyances of life, we are well on our way to a greater degree of happiness. And I suspect, we're unlikely to feel like we're spending one and one-half years standing in line at the Bureau of Motor Vehicles.

Overview of Section 3

Take Care of Yourself

WE ALL KNOW about the narcissists — those who are supremely self-centered; the person who constantly brings attention to him or herself, the person who lives to indulge his or her own pleasures. Such excesses are obvious to even the casual observer. Not so distinct are those on the other end of the continuum — those who stand more in the shadows and tend not to take care of themselves.

It is surprising how often people fail to take care of themselves. Whether it's their physical or mental health or their personal integrity, all too many fail to attend to what is best for their well being. Part of the difficulty lies in the fact that we are prone to attend to immediate desires instead of long term needs. Be it the unhealthy food or beverage in front of us versus the well being of our body, or the immediate pleasure of a leisure activity versus attending to family or friend matters, it's easy to lose sight of what's most important.

Because of the excesses of the selfish few, taking care of yourself has been given a bad name. I am not encouraging you to indulge yourself to the max. Rather the message is that attention to your personal mental and physical health as a top priority is critical to your happiness and well being and will ultimately benefit others around you.

CHAPTER 21

Take Care of Yourself

It's been my experience that people are a bit inconsistent when it comes to taking care of themselves. On the one hand, we work to avoid pain and to maximize happiness in the moment. Yet, on the other hand, in the big picture of life, many fail to take care of themselves.

Many years ago I had an office across from a family therapist. Among the various things he preached one stood out — to take care of yourself first. His argument was that you are the only person who is guaranteed to be there for the rest of your life. And secondly, when you take care of yourself, you are in a stronger position to take care of those around you.

This seemingly logical position often met with vigorous resistance. "Do you mean to say that I should put myself before my children, my spouse and my parents?" My friend would answer with a resounding "Yes". He advocated having priorities. Take care of yourself first, your spouse or partner second and your children third. At which point, you might hear some parent howl that they could never put their children's welfare behind their own.

Parental resistance is particularly understandable since children are dependent upon others. Their vulnerability definitely requires attention and support. But this therapist was not speaking of neglecting those needs or the needs of vulnerable older parents, but focusing on doing what is best for yourself and others in the long term.

His argument is analogous to building a strong foundation for a home. Marriages and parenting are both most successful when there is a strong underpinning. When you are happy and confident, those around you are more likely to be happy and confident.

Think, for a second, how many children are hindered when raised in a dysfunctional household. By contrast a strong, loving home is perhaps the greatest gift a mother and father can give to their children.

The resistance to my therapist friend's point of view also comes from those who hear his message as not providing love. That is not the message. The message is to take care of yourself as the top priority and then sufficiently and lovingly care for others.

In my clinical work, I have most often come across individuals who go to the extreme of putting others excessively before their own well being. Let me give you an example. Many years ago, while working in a pain clinic, a "little old lady" with serious back pain came to be treated. What was unusual was that her adult children carried her favorite chair as she walked down the hall and everywhere she went. Whenever she stopped, the chair was ready and she sat.

Her medical diagnosis was clear: severe muscular pain aggravated by inactivity and excessive time in this chair. Her treatment recommendations were clear as well: extensive graduated physical therapy including the removal of the chair so lovingly provided by her children.

Upon the last recommendation, the family strongly objected. "After all the years of love and attention given by our devoted mother, you are telling us that we should stop caring for her?" they angrily responded. Our attempts to assuage their anger failed. They abruptly left the clinic.

This reaction was common in the family therapy classes that I facilitated for many years — caretakers who excessively helped a family member to the point of personal burnout, some reaching a point of outright resentment. They, too, resisted taking care of themselves first, mistakenly believing we wished them to forsake caring for their loved one.

Excessive caretaking is just one example of not taking care of yourself, of not looking at the whole picture. Making sure you take care of your physical and mental health as a top priority, is critical throughout life. My therapist friend, standing on his soapbox, was providing a valuable life lesson.

CHAPTER 22

Respect Yourself

RESPECTING YOURSELF SEEMS such an obvious assertion that it feels silly to say. Yet, in my many years of doing therapy, I frequently observe clients whose actions indicate a lack of self-respect. Even more surprising is that they initially don't see it that way. Let me give an example.

Alice is a kind woman in her early thirties who possesses excellent social skills and work habits. Nevertheless, when it comes to her older sister, she allows herself to be verbally and emotionally abused. She hears insults such as "Given your looks, what can you expect?" Or humiliating remarks stated in public like, "I wouldn't trust my sister with that, she doesn't do anything right." Such assertions are outlandish, but Alice takes them in stride. A long discourse could follow as to why she allows such mistreatment, but at its heart is her lack of her self-worth. Her inability to stand up for herself starts with personal assumptions. She believes that standing up risks additional criticism and therefore is not worth the effort. She's just not worth it.

When individuals allow others to directly or indirectly damage their personal integrity or dignity they are not respecting themselves. They lack the courage to stand up for themselves, at least in some situations with some people.

It is not just those who are abused who show a lack of self-respect. It's the depressed or chronically sad individuals who lack the initiative to take control of their lives; the individual who cares for others to excess at the cost of their own health; the spouse whose partner does not allow them to express their thoughts and opinions or controls their behavior. In all of these cases, we see a lack of self-respect, an unwillingness to stand up for their worth. The hard truth is that a person who does not stand up for their rights is rationalizing. They are making an excuse to avoid the risk of criticism, rejection or potential loss.

There are numerous reasons to work on regaining self-respect. Respecting yourself is a wonderful thing. Those who respect themselves are happier and more confident. Such individuals are more prone to be kind to others, kindness not motivated by a need to be liked or to please, but a wish to give to others. Those who lack self-esteem and self-respect, on the other hand, contribute to a never-ending cycle of worry about measuring up.

I'm obviously biased in recommending work with a therapist to build your self-esteem. Altering one's self-perception is hard. Individuals often make temporary gains in replacing old beliefs with new ones, but sustaining such changes is difficult. Outside support and guidance can make a critical difference.

In my opinion respecting yourself should be your highest priority. Many people take better care of possessions like their car or their clothes than themselves. Still others put the needs of their loved ones before their own — a seemingly admirable behavior that is *undesirable in the long run*. "Respect yourself" is a simple suggestion that can change your life. It should be taken seriously.

Exercise

Respect Yourself Along Your Path

Every once in a while, it's worthwhile to examine whether you are truly taking care of yourself. A good place to begin is to examine daily behaviors and close relationships by the measure of self-respect.

1. Are you respecting yourself in how you manage your physical health? If not, what can you do? List it below.

2. Are you respecting yourself in how you manage your relationships? For example, acting assertively in expressing your needs. Write out what you need to do in order to feel self-respect in your relationships.

3. What are the steps that would be evidence to you that are respecting yourself in general? For example, taking time for yourself each day. Write out your actions.

CHAPTER 23

Loneliness, Not Something to Passively Accept

MY FATHER WAS a gregarious fellow — a master punster with his word play, followed by a well-timed Bob Newhart pause. In his elder years he would easily amuse people at the mall or in a grocery or hardware store with his charm and wit — a behavior that might make a teenager wince but always caused me to stand in awe.

Those are among the happy memories of my dad. The unhappy ones have to do with the loneliness he experienced in his old age. He was of the generation that wanted to die in their home, and this was a major factor in his isolation. Attempts to lure him to live with us, 1000 miles away from his home state, were as unsuccessful as they were understandable. Nor was the attraction of assisted living, with its many recreational opportunities and panoply of new "victims" for his latest jokes. Dad got his wish and stayed in his home until the end, but he paid a big price — chronic loneliness, despite regular visits from health care workers. The other hours were long and generally empty.

People can be unhappy in a wide variety of manners. But there is one that stands out — loneliness. Not the occasional bout of feeling lonely but chronic loneliness.

Loneliness is not difficult to detect. Lack of social contact and intimacy brings about emptiness and awareness that we are missing something critical to our well being. The very rare hermit notwithstanding, we are social animals. Individually we probably would not have survived as a species. But when we came together as families and communities, humankind flourished. Group life is now an element in our gene pool. Like food, when it is undersupplied, we decline.

Of course, everyone is lonely at some time in his or her life. It's a normal feeling — after a divorce, a breakup, loss of a loved one or a job, a move to a new city — any of these can prompt a feeling of isolation. *Chronic* loneliness is something else entirely. It can be devastating.

I will venture to say that chronic loneliness even contributes to violence — not the most common outcome for the lonely, but still a significant minority worth mentioning. Little attention has been paid to the fact that virtually all of the serial killers in the United State over the last two decades have been isolated and friendless young males. Such a mental environment lends itself to blaming others, intense anger, conspiracy theories, and a need for revenge. Most often the violence is taken out on themselves.

A ghastly consequence of chronic isolation is suicide, for which the United States ranks near the top among developed countries. More Americans die by their own hand than in car accidents, and gun suicides are almost twice as common as gun homicides.

Of course, chronic loneliness doesn't usually result in such extreme actions, but it is still very damaging. On a physical basis, one effect of chronic loneliness is that it undermines the body's ability to regulate the circulatory system, thus causing the heart to work harder. It negatively affects sleep, a major element in our health. Behaviorally and psychologically, chronic loneliness is very often a precursor to depression and alcoholism, and recent research lends credence to loneliness as a contributor to dementia.

All of this is to say that chronic loneliness is not something to take lightly. If a person were diagnosed with diabetes, no sensible person would ignore this information. Chronic loneliness is of the same magnitude and should be taken just as seriously.

Psychologist John Cacioppo, an expert on the long-term effects of loneliness, says that chronic loneliness establishes a "slowly unfolding pathophysiological process," a resulting wear and tear on the body and mind.[12]

For the chronically lonely, solving the problem may be like pushing mud upstream. Resistance may include shyness or excuses pertaining to health issues, finances, etc. Whatever the reasons, the need to overcome loneliness should be paramount. The alternative is very costly. As with my dad, every attempt may not be successful, but it is worth the effort to try very, very hard.

---

12 Cacioppo, J. and William, P., Loneliness: Human Nature and the Need for Social Connection, W.W. Norton & Co., New York, NY, 2008.

CHAPTER 24

Flaws and All

I CRACKED A coffee mug yesterday. Not just any mug but one I've had for over 25 years. One that has nurtured me on cold winter days and when my heart was heavy.

In Japan there is a technique to repair pottery called Kintsugi that mixes gold, silver or platinum dust with lacquer. The Japanese have expanded Kintsugi beyond a repair method into a philosophy that venerates repaired objects as ones having enhanced character and value. This viewpoint overlaps with another Japanese philosophy, wabi-sabi, which celebrates the flawed or imperfect. Both approaches value keeping an object around even after it has broken, highlighting the breaks and repairs as events in life, embracing cracks as part of existence.

In the human realm the acceptance of perceived flaws is difficult. We expect perfection. It's hard to recognize that we are in any way flawed.

Many years ago while in graduate school, I took my lunch in a greenhouse next to our academic building. Entering one blustery winter day I was astonished by the size of the enormous coleus before me. These vigorous plants, I was told, were the ones that had survived an earlier power outage and the accompanying low temperatures. It seems that they had been hardened by their stress, a common process in the plant world.

Power outages in life take many forms — unemployment, financial issues, major illnesses — whatever the experiences, we all have personal losses. We struggle through these difficulties, but it is those who learn from challenges who are stronger — much like coleus that survives harsh temperatures.

Our strength is even greater, when we recognize personal failings — the cracks, so to speak — in our personal makeup. Recognition of imperfections moves us toward emotional maturity. It opens the door to empathy and modesty. Empathy, by way of awareness that we all share imperfections, like bad habits, addictions, feelings of inadequacy, etc., etc. Empathy in realizing that everyone else struggles as well, appearances to the contrary.

Recognizing our flaws also fosters modesty regarding our own accomplishments. When complimenting friends, I often hear that they would not have been successful without their spouse and friends, an implicit awareness that personal inadequacies need assistance.

Recognition of personal flaws can be considered the first step. A second step toward maturity is the acceptance of those imperfections. Of course acceptance does not preclude efforts to overcome them. As humans we may never fully overcome our "cracks," but the effort is worthwhile. Nevertheless, like the technique of Kintsugi, the first step is repair. Like the philosophy of wabi-sabi, the second step is acceptance, flaws and all.

When we recognize our imperfections, work to repair them and then accept our imperfections, we go a long way toward a comfort with the complex "pottery" that we are. Accepting the cracks and repairs is wonderful in a coffee cup. It's even better when we do the same to ourselves. When we do, we can be as unique as the hardened and glorious coleus.

CHAPTER 25

Mindful of Everyday Pleasures

HAVING REWARDING EXPERIENCES is integral to our happiness, but determining what is a reward is actually a very complicated matter. What is a reward to one person may be a punishment to another. The idiom, "One man's meat is another man's poison," states it well.

The importance of having the right reward was illustrated in a class I taught early in my professional life called *Behavior Modification of the Mentally Retarded*.[13] A major assignment for the students in my class was to write a program that would teach a mentally slow child to learn an activity of daily living. But let me give you a little background before I expand upon one of the fascinating aspects of the children's learning experience.

If you were to go into institutions housing severely mentally retarded children in the 1950 and 60's, you might be shocked by how little the children did for themselves. At that time such children were considered unteachable and were totally dependent on others for every aspect of their lives. The 1970's brought an extraordinary and greatly underreported revolution — the extensive use of techniques to educate and train these children to feed and clothe themselves as well as take care of their basic hygiene.

---

13 The term, mentally retarded, is dated and may be unintentionally offensive. Current, more appropriate, terms may be intellectually challenged or intellectually disabled. The children with whom my students were serving were children who had severe inability to manage activities of daily living such as putting on a coat or eating with a fork and spoon.

The college campus where I taught had a special education program for such children and my job, in part, was to teach undergraduates to write behavior modification programs that would aid these children in learning everyday life skills. Additionally the "lab" portion of my course entailed my college students observing and learning the intricacies of the everyday experience of children in the special education class. One of the most fascinating aspects of this very worthwhile program was what the young children did at the beginning of each day.

Each morning, as the children arrived, they were taken individually into a "rewards" room where there were a myriad of small articles that the children might find pleasurable — tactile materials such as feathers, cushions, soft sponges; fragrant items such as perfumes and aromatic flowers; and audible bits such as brief sounds of music and toys, etc. From these hundreds of potential rewards, each child chose their three preferences for the day.

Throughout the day the child then received his or her reward immediately after exhibiting any small improvement in learning new behaviors. Each reward might be given dozens and dozens of times (that's why they had be very small and finite) and a different reward was given when the first one lost its reinforcing power. To give you an idea of the effort necessary, educating a child to put on a winter coat might take two months and thousands of rewards, but, of course, the child would then have that skill for the rest of his life — an enormous step in expanding an otherwise greatly limited life.[14]

It is worth stating that the children came to school each day eagerly and by all outward appearances found their experience exciting and, dare I say, very "rewarding."

---

14 It is important to note that the activities taught, such as putting on your clothes independently, become in time, their own reward. Once the children left the school environment they retained those skills with the proper support from their parents.

As I reflect upon the special education class, I am reminded of one of my favorite quotes from Benjamin Franklin: "Human happiness comes not from infrequent pieces of good fortune, but from the small improvements of daily life."

These children did not have to receive a grand prize, a seismic gift, to bring smiles to their faces. Receiving frequent small daily rewards resulted not only in learning but also created excitement, great pleasure and an eagerness to come to school. We, in turn, need not be dependent upon the "infrequent piece of good fortune" to gain a measure of well being but should attend to the little good fortunes that are around us if only we notice. And we don't have to go to a special "reward" room to get them.

Exercise

Look Around as You Travel Toward Happiness

Mindful of everyday pleasure is a sure way to maintain a high level of happiness. But there is another truism that comes from the science of positive psychology — the concept that we acclimate to positive experiences over time. Many everyday pleasures are taken for granted. They lose their novelty and move from our conscientiousness. Consequently it is beneficial to do the work of heightening the awareness of those items and events that may be commonplace, but valuable in our life.

One simple means to do this is to ask how we would feel if such an item were not available. For example how would you feel if you did not have your morning cup of coffee, the access to a hot shower, clothes, your car or transportation, etc? Even more important are questions related to the kindnesses of family and friends.

For the next seven days remind yourself of the gratefulness you feel for having any of the following:

Morning coffee or other beverage
Hot shower
Your transportation
Your clothes
Health
Write out any others you would like to list:

CHAPTER 26

Acceptance and Perspective, Not Perfection

I IMAGINE THAT Mahatma Gandhi was a bear to live with. Oh sure, there is that role he played in gaining India's independence, but I'm talking about his day-to-day life. The routine salt enema he gave himself for forty straight years. And weaving may be interesting for a while but, personally, done every day I doubt that it would wear well (no pun intended).

I've always been fascinated by the details of the lives of great men and women of history. Part of my intrigue is that I assume the grand stories tend to leave out the foibles of our admired brothers and sisters. And that's the part, to me, that makes them human, their flaws woven into their fabric of greatness. Indeed, I'd like to read a book entitled "The Defects of Great Men and Women"— a book that would make these people real.

What does this have to do with happiness? A great deal if you consider that perspective and acceptance are valuable assets in dealing with personal issues. If we were to realize that the most astounding humans, those humans who have accomplished unbelievable feats, are as flawed as we are, then we can be a little more accepting of our own deficiencies. One of my favorite stories along these lines concerns John Quincy Adams. In his mid-life John Quincy Adams wrote in his diary:

> "I am forty-five years old. Two-thirds of a long life have passed, and I have done nothing to distinguish it by usefulness to my country and to mankind."

This is a man who at the time of this writing had held the following offices: Minister to the Hague, Emissary to England, Minister to Prussia, State Senator, United States Senator, Minister to Russia, Head of the American Mission to negotiate peace with England, Minister to England, Secretary of State, member of the House of Representatives and President of the United States. Close to his death at age eighty, John Quincy Adams wrote somberly in his diary:

> "My whole life has been a succession of disappointments. I can scarcely recollect a single instance of success in anything I have ever undertook."[15]

John Quincy Adams is a prime example of how our internal perceptions are the real agents behind our feelings. If his extraordinary achievements can't create a sense of success, then it's hard to imagine what could. But, of course, the lesson is, once again, that it is not the events of the world that create our feelings, it is our interpretation of the events. Given the filter that John Quincy Adams brought to the table, apparently no accomplishment brought him lasting satisfaction.

Be it Mother Teresa, Nelson Mandela, Harry Truman, Ronald Reagan, Abraham Lincoln, Eleanor Roosevelt, or the Dali Lama, a close examination of each life reveals deficiencies.

John Quincy Adams wrestled with depression. It is no wonder. If one's personal happiness is built on external accomplishments and a standard so high as to court ridicule, it is likely to be fragile. Better that we look to our strengths, accept our imperfections, and understand that even the best of humanity is peppered with flaws. Better

---

15 Barden, C., *Meet the Presidents*, Lorenz Educational Press, Payton, Ohio, 2009

not to follow the mental filter of John Quincy Adams. It is often hard to be forgiving when we look critically at our own failings. It is even harder to be accepting. But these qualities are important in maintaining a sense of well being.

CHAPTER 27

Worthy Enough to Speak Up

MANY YEARS AGO I carried a little piece of paper stuffed in my wallet on which was written one word — "assertive." The word was a reminder that I needed to address an absent behavior — speaking up for my needs and wants. It's not that I was a pansy, with people walking over me. It was more that I walked away from conversations thinking, "I should have said this or that" and often didn't feel good about the way I'd handled things.

Many years have passed and my own assertiveness skills have become greatly enhanced, but I find that many of my clients have a similar issue. Often their lack of assertiveness is accompanying by a lack of self-esteem and a feeling that they are not controlling the world but are being controlled by it.

A dramatic example of this feeling occurred in a woman I treated for chronic severe headaches — so severe that she'd had many teeth removed and multiple operations on her jaw. She was also addicted to narcotic pain medication. By the time I saw her she had been to over a dozen specialists, all to no avail.

Her story is quite interesting and instructive. The patient was very small in stature, barely five feet tall, and thin. She spoke in a soft voice and avoided eye contact, an indication of very low self-esteem. This was corroborated by her many self-deprecating remarks and body posture. But, perhaps, most revealing was the story of her relationship with her husband, a very large man, a CEO who travelled internationally and dealt with corporate empires.

Her husband was authoritarian and very traditional in his perception of a strong man. His ran a "tight ship" in his business and expected the same of his wife in her duties as a housewife and mother. Consequently, her children had to be perfect and her floors, as the saying goes, clean enough to eat off. A critical issue in understanding the wife's condition was knowing that the husband never revealed when he would arrive home at the end of the day or even from trips. As a result his wife was in a constant state of tension, evidenced especially in the muscles in her upper back and skull.

An obvious solution to her headaches was for her to leave her husband and thus her stressful situation. However, the husband did, in fact, love his wife deeply. He had no idea that he was in any way a factor in her tension or headaches. She, too, would not think of leaving her husband, for in her eyes, he was a caring father, a good provider and a loving husband.

To me, the real problem was that the woman was a "pleaser." She had an extreme lack of self-esteem, was unassertive and avoided conflict at any cost. In her effort to never fail and to maintain an immaculate home absent of any imperfection, she was, in everyday language, a nervous wreck.

Her poor self-esteem fed her fear of her husband's judgment and made her even more unable to speak up for her own wants and needs. Her inability to assert herself caused her to swallow her husband's behaviors without communicating the stress that she was undergoing. The combination of her need to please and to avoid conflict created muscular tension so extreme that she endured severe headaches for over a decade.

Although this woman is an extreme case, I have found that unassertiveness and poor self-esteem often go hand in hand. Internal dialogs are filled with beliefs that the right to speak up is not as important as others' needs, that speaking up would be useless or that getting into a conflict is too painful. These and similar thoughts result in the feeling I spoke of earlier, not being in control of one's life — a quite unhappy feeling.

When my headache client went through therapy, she was able to change some of her self-talk, particularly the appropriateness of speaking up without being aggressive, and she found her bodily tension and her headaches greatly diminished.

You may find the above story interesting, but wonder how it relates to well being and happiness. There is a truism in the world of positive psychology that research has abundantly supported. Simply put, our internal dialog and the assumptions we make about ourselves are key to our well being and happiness.

Dialog is at its healthiest when filled with self-confidence and self-respect — self-respect built on the belief that our own needs are worthy of expression.

Those with self-confidence and the ability to express their own wishes know that they will not get their way all the time. But they also know that they can feel better about themselves when they express their own wishes in a fair and balanced fashion.

Sometimes we need a little reminder to practice behaviors that may produce a greater sense of well being and happiness — something as simple as carrying a slip of paper with the word "assertive" written on it.

Exercise

Be Assertive as You Travel

In any discussion of assertiveness it is important to distinguish assertiveness from aggression. Aggressive behavior is that which harms another, while assertiveness is a form of expressing oneself in a forceful, confident manner with no intention or effort to harm another. Indeed the lack of assertiveness is often harm to yourself not another.

Assertiveness is based on the assumption that each of us has a right to our opinions, our dignity and respect. Examine the following questions and assess whether you need to work on becoming more assertive.

1. Do you fail to speak up because you feel your opinions are not worthwhile?

2. Do you fail to speak up because you fear you will be criticized?

3. Do you feel like other people consistently limit your behavior?

4. Do you feel emotionally abused by another person?

5. Do you feel that you are often insulted by another person or persons?

6. Do you feel that it is not your right to express your needs?[16]

---

16 If you answer affirmatively to more than one of the above questions you should seriously consider working on your self-esteem, confidence and assertiveness. Consider searching out self-help books on these topics and modeling friends who are confident and assertive, or seek professional help.

CHAPTER 28

Completing Those Little Onerous Tasks

I'M A RELATIVELY orderly person whose office sometimes disintegrates into disarray and low levels of dirt. But, after a recent thorough office straightening, I marveled at the degree of pleasure I felt and wondered, with all of the major issues in life bubbling around me, how I could feel such enjoyment over something as simple as cleaning my office. Why is that so? And since it feels so good, why don't I do it more often?

The reality is that some tasks are low priorities. "A few things out of place won't hurt." "Nobody's going to see it." "I've got other things to do that are more important." It's this type of thinking that allows us to procrastinate about a whole series of activities: getting a medical exam, cleaning the car or writing an overdue note. Of course some people like to do these activities, but a large number of us tend to put them off for another day.

On the other hand, some low priority activities jump to the top when an even more onerous task shows up. My office gets a good straightening when my taxes are due. Some people can carry this avoidance to the extreme.

An acquaintance of mine was a prime example. This woman would carefully peruse the want ads each morning (another era) for a much-needed job. But instead of immediately following up on prospective employment opportunities, she would circle her preferences in red pen. The following day she would type them out on 3X5 cards and prioritize them. She contacted the employer on the third day, only to find that she was at the end of a line of applicants. When she finally landed a job, she would further exhibit her ambiguity regarding work by frequently being late and getting fired, only to start the circular process once again.

Most of us are not so obsessive, but we avoid doing certain tasks, building up tension the longer the work goes undone. That's one of the reasons we enjoy completing the task at long last — reducing the tension by knowing that the task is done and believing that it won't have to be done again for a while.

Of course, there are other rewards as well. Completing tasks such as straightening the office means that things are back where they belong and I'm ready to work — a clean desk, pens in their cup and books in their place. Why is that important? I suspect it has to do with a feeling of certainty — comfort that I know where things are and can get to them efficiently.

All of this is to say I enjoy having a straightened and clean office. You may feel the same about a kitchen, bedroom, car, lawn or attic. Some tasks, however, need to be done time and time again. But you do still feel a temporary sense of gratification as you accomplish your task. Why let the pleasure fade? You don't have to immediately redo the task. Savor its completion. Sit and admire it. Relish it. There is great reward in luxuriating in the little pleasures of everyday life.

CHAPTER 29

Your Bucket List

MANY YEARS AGO I received a postcard I still treasure. It was from a woman traveling in Europe celebrating her wonderful trip — a woman I hardly knew, but it nevertheless touched my heart.

The woman, probably in her early seventies, had come to a presentation I gave on dealing with pain and living well. After the presentation she joined a group of attendees who asked questions, but she lingered so we could talk in private.

She told me that she had recently been diagnosed with an advanced stage of cancer and was uncertain how to spend her remaining time. I asked her if there was anything she regretted not doing in her life and, without hesitation, she said she had always wanted to travel to Europe.

My presentation had promoted the importance of taking care of yourself and that, when done with some consideration, it is not only the best thing that you can do for yourself, but those around you. The underlying message was clear: when you are happy you are most likely to be kind and generous to the people you love. Given that message, my response was firm. "By all means follow your dream. You've wanted to go the Europe all your life but always put it off. This is the time to do it. Would you rather die at home or travelling in Europe with your husband?" She chose the latter. Two months later I received the postcard, "Thank you so very much."

Her question seemed simple — what to do with the rest of her life. But, of course, it doesn't feel simple to most people. In her case she still had to consider what medications she would need, her stamina and the impact on those around her.

Choosing what to do with your life and how to do it is something many struggle with. Life coaches, commencement speakers and parents are quick to give inspirational recommendations. My suggestion is more mundane and perhaps more difficult. It is to periodically sit down and write out whatever comes to mind regarding your life desires and then take steps, even tiny ones, to reach those goals.

Here are some questions that can help you to think a little deeper on the subject. What do you most fear losing? Your fears, just as much as your desires, reveal what is most important in your life. If you fear being alone, or losing a loved one, you might want to think about taking action to cement your other relationships further. Set up a plan with specific actions and attack it just as conscientiously as you might set out to land a job, get an education or arrange your finances. Relationships are certainly as important as any of those.

What makes your heart beat with excitement? Sure, living on an exotic island, winning the lottery or other glamorous things, but erased those from your list. They are probably pretty much outside of your control. On the other hand, there may be some that are difficult to pull off, like the trip to Europe for this woman, but are still plausible. These should definitely be given thorough consideration. Maybe they're not as impossible as you've previously thought.

Another useful exercise is to imagine yourself 5, 10 or 15 years older than you are now. What would you like to have accomplished in those years? What would you regret not having done? These, too, need to be given serious thought. Analyzing small steps that can move you toward your desired goal is a good way to start.

I'm a big fan of personal mission statements. I've written many, revising and returning to them periodically — often during times of uncertainty. They have helped ground me, reminding me what is most important in my life. In that sense they have helped me to regroup, even energized me to return to long-term challenges. Choosing goals that resonate with your deepest personal values and talents, whether you succeed or not, are likely to be worth the effort.

No matter what your age, there are things that can be done. Even dying well, as Morrie Swartz of *Tuesdays With Morrie* fame and others have shown us, can provide purpose.[17] Bucket lists are fun in movies. They're even better if they're yours, and you have given serious thought to fulfilling them.

---

17 Albom, M., *Tuesdays with Morrie: An Old Man, a Young Man, and Life's Greatest Lesson*, Random House, New York, NY, 1997.

CHAPTER 30

Embrace Sadness

A RECENT DISNEY movie, *Inside Out*, did an extraordinary thing — it celebrated sadness. The plot, simple enough: an 11-year-old girl deals with the stresses of her family's move from Minnesota to San Francisco. What makes the movie interesting is that most of the story takes place inside the girl's head.

Familiar aspects of consciousness, Joy, Disgust, Anger, Sadness and Fear — all animated characters — play their roles. Faced with the stresses of new peers, uncertainty, isolation and new landscapes, the emotions battle for dominance in a fashion we all know. Joy attempts to be the guiding force, since the girl has always been a happy person, but her frustrations are fueled by Anger and Fear, even a bit of Disgust. But most importantly, as we all know in facing loss, Sadness plays a major role. This development turns especially relevant when Sadness turns out not to be Joy's rival but rather her friend, and ultimately the most notable and poignant emotion.

Sadness, as a hero, is not often seen in Disney movies or for that matter in many films. But sadness is indeed a real emotion that needs to be recognized as crucial for our humanity and well being. Sadness is necessary if the word happiness is to have any meaning.

Sadness is a vector: that is, it facilitates a multitude of admirable feelings and behaviors, such as honor, empathy and kindness. Most importantly, it is by acknowledging sadness that we connect with others at a meaningful level.

The sadness we feel over the death of a friend is likely to be accompanied by reminisces of happy times together. In all probability we will take some action that honors our lost friend and share our feelings with others — behaviors that bring communities together. It may even cause us to contemplate our own mortality and take action to feed our legacy.

Seeing others less fortunate than ourselves, we express our sadness with empathy and, in the best of circumstances, take action. Kindness, volunteer work and general charity often have sadness as their starting point.

In *Inside Out*, the character Sadness ultimately causes the little girl to reveal her innermost thoughts and worries to her parents. When they, too, share their sadness over what they have lost in their move from Minnesota, a core family experience transpires. The character Joy could never have brought the family together the way an honest expression of sadness did.

We need sadness. It's a fundamental human experience. It makes happiness and joy possible. Embrace it. Reveal it. Share your feelings with close friends and loved ones. It is a major failing to hide our sadness from loved ones.

Sadness has its problems, of course. When allowed to linger without action it can grow into depression. When hopelessness and despair enter the picture, we can get into trouble. But given these cautions, sadness is not to be avoided. Experiencing sadness for a limited time is to be human and, in its own way, is to be treasured.

Be Open to Sadness As You Travel

> There are as many nights as days, and the one is just as long
> as the other in the year's course. Even a happy life cannot be
> without a measure of darkness, and the word 'happy' would
> lose its meaning if it were not balanced by sadness.
>
> Carl Jung

The next time you are sad, note the time and day and hour during which your sadness began. Allow yourself to feel the experience
without criticism of the emotion, but also place a limit on the length
of time you settle into this sadness; for example one or two days.
Grief is different than sadness, and should be managed differently

Write out a recent time during which you were sad, noting the
circumstance and the length of your feelings.

Write down what benefit you experienced from your sadness. Here
are some possibilities: It expressed my love. I have a full range of
emotions including sadness and I am willing to experience it. I appreciate happiness more when I understand that sadness is a part of life.

CHAPTER 31

A Sure Fire Way to Increase Your Happiness

Cleaning up the trash on a beach or roadside, joining a committee or board of a non-profit organization, acting as a child advocate, serving food at a homeless shelter, listening to families at Hospice, being a greeter at a church — the list goes on and on. The areas in which my friends volunteer could fill a page, some tasks requiring skill and talent, others simply time and a good heart.

When you search the literature for behaviors that strongly promote happiness, volunteering jumps out. About a quarter of Americans do just that — volunteer on a regular basis. No wonder. The common refrain "I get so much more than I give" is authentically felt. In just one confirmation, neuroscientist David Linden detailed how the brain's pleasure center is activated by generous behaviors towards others. But that's just the beginning. Volunteering benefits physical health and is associated with reduced mortality risk, especially for people age 60 and over. Then there's the sense of purpose, improved social support, reinforcement of a positive self-image and a greater degree of overall happiness. It's no wonder that so many people volunteer.

At the heart of volunteering is reaching out to others, but it can do much more. There is a story of a grieving woman who goes to a wise man for advice. Her husband had died tragically the previous year and she continued to be in deep mourning. The wise man tells her that he has no magic potions or pills for her grief but that her recovery can come about if she finds someone who is very happy and without any sorrow of their own. He counsels her that she must listen very carefully to what they say if she is to move past her grief.

The woman begins her quest in her rural village by going to the top of a nearby hill where the wealthy people live. However, as soon as she inquires about the happiest person in the household, she is immediately told of the problems and sorrow present. She listens carefully but finds nothing that soothes her grief and continues onto the next house. In each home she finds the same. Every home is a mixture of happiness and sorrow or mostly problems. After many homes, however, she notices that her own sadness begins to lessen.

Variations of this story exist in many cultures. Grieving and sorrow are appropriate. They tend to overstay their welcome, however, if kept totally inside. The woman in the story gave to others by listening and they, unknowingly, helped to distract her from her own troubles. Moreover, she began to gain meaning in her life as well as increase her contact with other people. Most everyone feels happier when they are with other people and even more so when they feel a sense of connection.

The story also illustrates two other features embedded in volunteer activity — kindness and perspective — features that contribute mightily to a strong sense of well being. Acts of kindness bolster happiness by activating the brain's pleasure center mentioned above. It also generates a feeling of accomplishment. There's the added attraction of fostering reciprocal acts of kindness and certainly gratitude from others — valuable happiness assets.

If that were not enough, most volunteering is provided to others less fortunate and thus likely to stimulate a sense of perspective, awareness that we have much to be grateful for.

There is one other observation I have about my friends who volunteer as a part of their life — they tend to be very happy people.

CHAPTER 32

Feeling Needed

FEELING NEEDED IS a core element in happiness and well being. We see it in those who do volunteer work and in those who take care of a loved one and, although it's demanding, wouldn't have it any other way. We see it in those with a special talent that benefits others and who take joy in their activity even without financial gain.

An extraordinary example of this is illustrated in the book, *Being Mortal: Medicine and What Matters in the End*, Atul Gawande's best-selling testimonial to the importance of maintaining quality of life as long as possible.[18] In the many stories he relates, that of Dr. Bill Thomas stands out. After spending his early medical years as an emergency room physician, the innovative doctor found himself the head of a nursing home, "a facility with 80 severely disabled elderly residents." What he also found was despair, in both the patients and the staff, in a culture that was based solely on organizational rather than human needs.

His solution was radical and ingenious. To open-mouthed staff members, Dr. Thomas pushed bringing dogs and cats into the facility. Two dogs and four cats to be exact. Not as occasional visitors, but as full time residents. While the staff was adjusting, worrying how they would handle care of these new residents, Dr. Thomas upped the ante and recommended introducing birds to the nursing

---

18 Awande, A.G., *Being Mortal: Medicine and What Matters in the End*, Henry Holt and Co., New York, NY, 2014

home —- 100 birds. As one astonished staff member recalled, "ONE HUNDRED BIRDS! IN THIS PLACE? You've got to be out of your mind! Have you ever lived in a house that has two dogs and four cats and 100 birds?"

What happened next is detailed in Dr. Thomas' own book, but the short of it is that patients who had been lethargic, bored and depressed by the everyday routine that had taken away their autonomy, began volunteering to take the dogs for a walk. They wanted to be responsible for changing cat litter and cleaning bird cages — to do anything that allowed them to once again feel needed in some small way. Overall, both patient and staff satisfaction soared.

The essence of the story is that, in addition to wanting creature comforts, we all yearn to feel needed, to be of use, even in a small way. It provides us with a sense of identity. One reason that many early retirees feel lost is the absence of this feeling.

Many years ago a friend of mine visited India and came back with a bounty of pictures and stories, all of which I have forgotten — except one. The picture was of a courtyard with a beautiful lawn and two women, proud because they meticulously cut the lawn every day. That was their full-time job. Noteworthy because they cut this moderate size lawn with scissors. Putting aside the issues of efficiency and poverty in India for a moment, my friend spoke of the immense pleasure these two women had in their daily accomplishment.

Not feeling needed plays a role in virtually every area of mental malaise I can think of. Depression and anxiety are substantially worse when not offset by the satisfaction of feeling needed, of having a purpose in life. Addictions of all kinds, certainly including alcohol abuse, are very often a cover up for the absence of feeling needed. Self-esteem is bolstered in those who feel needed and diminished in those who do not. Certainly the loss of employment immediately raises deep emotional reactions of not feeling needed, in addition to the many other issues caused by this stressor.

Grand standards don't have to be met for a person to feel needed. The most menial job can go a long way in reducing a sense of emptiness. Examining how and where you feel needed is worth your time. Count every possibility: caring for relatives, friends, animals, the environment and organizations. If the list is not to your liking, it may be time to take action.

In the nursing home example, it is wise to consider facilitating opportunities for the elderly to feel needed. The same applies to each of us.

CHAPTER 33

Men, A Word to the Wise

SAM IS ASTOUNDED by how long his wife talks on the phone. He's not alone. Most men are bewildered at the feat, and many are secretly envious. Women are not just outlasting their male counterparts in phone time, but also in sharing laughter and closeness. Men may joke about the time women are chatting about "nothing," but most understand that this is a well-established manner in which women bond.

This gender difference is not minor. Women have more friendships and deeper ones than men. And, not inconsequentially, women live significantly longer than men. A 2005 Australian longitudinal study of aging found that family relationships have little impact on longevity, while friendships increase life expectancy by as much as 22 percent.[19]

Men differ in whom they have for their closest relationships. It is most often with the opposite sex. When men do have male friendships, they generally stay away from sharing personal information and feelings and save such information for their women friends. Developmentally this makes sense. In their early years men are taught to hide emotions that might show weakness. Given the macho ethos of strength and competitiveness, closeness is viewed as dangerous. Whether one accepts this developmental assumption, there is no

---

19 *The Australian Longitudinal Study of Ageing* conducted at Finders University: A report of the Government of South Australia

doubt that men throughout the world have a greater tendency to compete with each other and a greater likelihood of hiding their emotions.

Another way that men differ is that women are taught to draw one another out, while men are not. Every woman knows, especially during their courting years, that enticing men to talk about themselves (it's easy) is a means of attracting their interest. This female skill allows women to enter personal information territory, an area most men find largely out of bounds. For many men, this is not considered manly.

The lack of close male friendship contributes to the higher frequency of deep depression in men upon divorce or the death of their wife. Men, more than women, place their emotional eggs in their spouse's basket. When their spouse leaves or dies, men find themselves feeling vulnerable. Their grieving period is shorter than women's, and their search to find a female replacement results in their tendency to remarry quicker.

Although most men do have male friends, their friendships are often based on mutual activities like sports or work. What they lack are *close* male friendships, intimate male friendships where they can share their fears and vulnerability and what is happening psychologically. It is here where we find the greatest benefits of relationships. It is here where the stresses of life find an outlet. Bottling up worries behind a wall of manliness is simply unhealthy.

Opportunities to make new friends are countless: interests and sports activities, clubs, churches and educational programs, volunteering and even forming a group of your own. The issue is not opportunity, but making the effort to spend time one-on-one to deeply connect. It is the latter effort that yields the most dividends. Once again, if we look at the women's world, we find that women's one-on-one time talking about personal matters exceeds that of men. Small luncheons and similar settings are where these interactions take place.

We men don't want to be women. But we might want to follow their example in our own way when we realize that it's a healthy and rewarding thing to do. Close friendships are too valuable a commodity to leave unnourished. Perhaps not on the phone, but in many other ways.

Overview of Section 4

Be Aware of Your Mental Habits

KNOWING AND DOING are two different things. We may understand that what we think largely controls how we feel, but fail to take action to manage our thinking. We may know that planning long-term goals is important, but taking the time to lay out a plan may elude us. We may know that taking care of ourselves is critical to our own happiness and those around us but fail to prioritize this critical action. We certainly agree that relationships are the most important things in our life but, again, allow time spent cementing and deepening relationships to fall behind less important behaviors. Too often, we attend to short-term actions and defer the attention to long-term goals that contribute to our happiness.

Building the habit of attending to our happiness is as critical as maintaining those behavioral habits that lead to a healthy body, arguably more so. Think of how often you have focused on eating better or doing more exercise or losing some weight, and compare that to the attentions you have given to increasing your sense of maturity or optimism on life. These perceptions and outlooks take effort to acquire, every bit as much as those actions needed to improve your physical health.

Without regular practice we are prone to "default" into mental distortions that defeat our journey toward well being and happiness. When we practice approaching life problems with balance, objectivity, perspective and self-compassion, we navigate life-challenges with a much better set of tools.

CHAPTER 34

A Mindset of Kindness

WHEN I TEACH classes on happiness, I regularly give students homework after each class. Homework such as: give five new compliments daily for 7 consecutive days, record three different things each day for which you are grateful, write down accomplishments that make you most proud, etc. Pretty straight forward, but surprising how each assignment gives a little happiness bump when done on a consistent basis.

Perhaps the most beneficial homework is the assignment to give five acts of kindness every day beyond your usual kind acts. This assignment forces students to look around, searching for opportunities to be kind. It creates a mindset. What follows is quite simple: a compliment, a favor or a small inconvenience in order to help another. Additionally, the giver receives pleasure from having taken the time to be kind.

When the class members share their homework, they regularly comment on how pleasant the effort is. Most remark that it is somewhat unfamiliar territory to actively search for opportunities to give five *additional* kindnesses every day, even though everyone believes themselves to be kind.

When I counsel those who claim to have poor self-esteem, I often ask them to state their positive characteristics. Most who lack self-confidence struggle with the question. However, if I ask directly whether they are kind, virtually everyone answers yes. Apparently all of us believe we are kind. It seems a major insult to be perceived as unkind.

How often we perform kind acts can be a rough measure of our emotional state. Happy people are most apt to be kind. Those who are sad, less so, but still capable of kindness. For those who are *mildly* depressed, a kind act is less probable. And for those who are truly depressed, kindness is likely to be rare. It is not that depressed people are inherently less kind; it is simply that depression narrows a person's focus to the dilemma that they feel. Their emotional energy is concentrated on their issues.

Ironically, being kind can reduce sadness. When we feel sad, it is beneficial to force ourselves to increase our kindness. Not only does it give us a sense of satisfaction, it also cements and expands our network of friends — valuable contributors to our well being.

One way to increase kindness frequency is to think of kindness as a privilege, to be on the lookout for opportunities to be kind. Think of a time when you were truly able to make a difference in someone's life with a kind act. What pleasure you likely provided both them and yourself! Such occasions are more probable if we create an attitude to make them happen.

The one caution I have is against thinking big. Small kindnesses are more readily available. Little opportunities occur most often. I suspect that most of us would rather be around those who fill our life with abundant kindnesses than with only the rare big kindness.

As silly as it may first appear, prompting ourselves to be kind may be wise. We can become so absorbed with daily activities that we fail to address this pillar of well being. Look for kindness opportunities. Such a habit can sustain a wonderful emotional state for you and those around you.

Exercise
The Best Guide to Keep on the Path to Happiness: Kindness

For 7 days, give yourself a check for each act of kindness beyond those you normally complete, making sure each kind act is different.

Day	Kindness 1	Kindness 2	Kindness 3	Kindness 4	Kindness 5
1					
2					
3					
4					
5					
6					
7					

CHAPTER 35

The Advantages of Being Vulnerable

THERE ARE MANY theories as to why we shake hands. A sign of friendship, sportsmanship, and trust are among the most common explanations. But, from an evolutionary standpoint, I like the idea that primitive man displayed that he had no weapon in his hand, allowing himself to be vulnerable. It's that vulnerability that intrigues me.

Being vulnerable is risky and can be frightening. Who wants that? But, then again, never being vulnerable carries many problems as well, especially in personal relationships and living life to the fullest.

One of my early career choices relates to stepping forward into vulnerability. I was terrified of speaking before groups but also aware that every occupation I considered suitable meant presenting myself in the public sphere. I chose to teach.

Now, many years later, I receive praise for my teaching. But when someone says, "You make it seem so effortless," I have to laugh to myself. They don't know the absolute terror I felt prior to walking into each and every class during my early years. They didn't see the sweat that poured down my back as I stood in front of the class reading my notes, eyes cemented to the paper. Or the agony I felt at the end of summer with the approach of the first day of class. I worked hard, but my story is not unique. Most everyone has his or her own version of high anxiety in the early stages of an endeavor. Those who faced their fear and worked through it, however, often have a wonderful payoff.

There is a reason that *Alcoholics Anonymous* open their meetings with "My name is ____ and I am an alcoholic." It sets the stage for everyone in the room to show their vulnerability, to lessen a hierarchy that might otherwise inhibit discussion and growth. It's well known in psychology circles that, if you want someone to open up regarding their personal life, a good approach is to share part of your own.

Virtually everyone knows that when they share news of an illness, tragedy, or death in their family, what follows is a short sympathetic acknowledgement of the loss and then a story about the listener's own challenges in a similar area. You never know how many broken limbs, heart attacks and loss of relatives there are until you share your story. Then your sense that you are alone in your particular difficulty is replaced by the ubiquity of it. The door to another people's personal life is often opened when we open our own. You allowed others to know you're subject to life's tragedies, and they, in turn, shared their experience. Vulnerability promotes vulnerability.

In the stereotypic picture of therapy the patient talks and the therapist listens. The patient has the problem and the therapist is the model of sanity, without depression or anxiety. In such a view the therapist has all the answers to life's difficulties. Reality is very different. Therapists struggle and work through life's trials, tribulations and tragedies every bit as much as others. Therapists have their personal demons too. My experience with clients is to frequently remind them that they need to work and practice good life management habits, just as I need to do the same. When I am open, honest and vulnerable, the client is as well. We make progress.

I'm not recommending that you share your personal life in a thoughtless fashion. It can be risky and off-putting. Doing so casually can be offensive. On the other hand, vulnerability is important in encouraging deep relationships, more prescribed for our inner circle and special circumstances. There it is crucial that we move past the banal exchanges of daily life and into deeper knowledge of each other. Risky perhaps, but the step necessary to gain close relationships.[20]

---

20 While the value of vulnerability is highlighted in this chapter, it is important to combine your openness with an ability to listen when others share personal stories. Finding friends who can reciprocate with vulnerability and listening skills may sometimes be difficult but worth pursuing.

CHAPTER 36

Accentuate the Positive

IF I WERE to compliment you ten times and insult you once, next month you'd probably remember the insult although you may have forgotten the compliments. We are programmed to register negatives more than positives. Negatives are hurtful and they stick. In troubled marriages where criticisms are commonplace, one partner often walks on eggshells, anticipating danger.

Print and electronic media are keenly aware of this sensitivity to negatives. Their first goal is to get our attention, and they know that "another nice day in paradise" won't draw many readers. We pay attention to the exciting, scandalous, outrageous and terrifying. Consequently, they deluge us with death and destruction.

Historically, it makes sense that we are more sensitive to the negative. From our primitive beginnings, those on alert were more likely to survive the dangers in their surroundings. Better to hear the quiet movements of a predator than to be eaten by it. People who were insensitive probably didn't live long enough to pass on their genes.

Although there is value in this alertness, it can also cause problems. Careers requiring intense focus on danger exact a penalty of increased levels of anxiety, depression and stress.

Interestingly, recent research shows how most people, not in careers requiring high alertness, adjust to sensitivity to the negative. They simply adapt a generally more optimistic attitude.

The study, reported in the *Proceedings of the National Academy of Sciences*, suggests that there is a *Universal Positivity Bias*: that is, a counterpoint to our tendency to accentuate the negative. People in virtually every corner of the world use more positive than negative words. While journalists and others seeking our attention may focus on the negative, the everyday chatter between friends, workers and acquaintances tally more upbeat words like "healthy, marriage, friends, tasty and exciting" than negatives like "idiot or ghastly."

The results make sense. While negatives do stand out, they do so in the presence of exponentially more everyday little and big positives. Murder and tragedy may temporarily stick in your mind, but good food, family, friends, and happy events consume a much greater portion of our personal conversation.

Having positive experiences isn't the only reason for greater occurrence of positive words. Researchers posited that greater use of those words is a way of offsetting the negative. "Look for the silver lining" appears to be a sound adage for good mental health and survival.

All of this is to say that we need to be aware of how we are hardwired. Our evolutionary legacy is to be alert to things negative, hostile and dangerous. But fortunately, our evolved brain has also developed a strategy to counter the negative bias — rationally attending to the positive events around us. Those who are optimistic and grateful for the myriad of life's good fortune seem to be the ones who benefit the most.

Exercise
Accentuate the Positive as You Move Forward

In accentuating the positive you naturally become more grateful, the two are intimately intertwined. Consequently accentuating the positive, and highlighting those experiences and things for which you are grateful, is a sure fire way to increase your happiness. Try it and see for yourself.

For the next seven days, write down three things for which you are grateful. Do not repeat items from day to day.

Day	Grateful Item	Grateful Item	Grateful Item
1			
2			
3			
4			
5			
6			
7			

Overview of Section 5

Don't Let the Demons Win

EVERYONE APPEARS TO have demons. They seem to be a part of our DNA. Like mosquitoes on a hot summer night they appear beyond our control. To be clear, I am not speaking of external, supernatural demons. I am speaking of internal, self-created irascible thoughts, worries, obsessions, inadequacies, and feelings of perceived failings. They unerringly appear during times of fearfulness and often fester in reoccurring dreams.

A naturalist friend tells me that mosquitoes have a significant role in evolution. They both provide food for birds and eliminate the weakest in herds of elk or antelope as well as other animals. Like mosquitoes, the negative qualities of demons stand out more than any positives. Demons create anxiety. They intensify feelings of inadequacy. They magnify fears. They seem beyond our control and are, thereby, immensely frustrating and damaging.

Let's take the common dream that leaves a person feeling embarrassed or lost. No expertise in dream analysis is needed to sense that the dreamer fears being found inadequate. The dreamer feels they he or she is wearing a mask and is afraid that an inadequate self might be revealed. Most everyone has such dreams occasionally, but when frequent and persistent, their inner demons have struck.

The hidden demons in dreams are no different than the more explicit deprecating statements we may make overtly such as "I can't do anything right," or "I'm less of a man or women because I can't do some specific manly or womanly thing." Demons often have a cohort, a "sidekick," in the damaging department — "shoulds." I *should* be smarter, thinner, taller, prettier, or handsomer, than I am. All contribute to a poorer self-esteem or worth than need be. When demons are around for a while, they can even show up in persistent headaches, shoulder or stomach aches.

Given their inherent harm, it is difficult to imagine how demons can in any way be beneficial. My hypothesis is that demons, like pain, act as a signal that work needs to be done. You may notice that demons have a habit of appearing most often when you are stressed or worried. They seem to know when you are most vulnerable, like pain that appears when you haven't taken care of your body. Demons appear more often when we are failing to do the work needed to maintain a good sense of self, the work of relationship skills or the "pillars" of happiness: gratitude, kindness and controlling what you can control.

In the physical realm we pretty much know what needs to be done to maintain a healthy body. We may be burdened with some inherent disability, but no matter what limitations, we have a sense of what actions need to be taken to make the most of what we have been given at birth. In the psychological realm the same applies. We may have dyslexia, anxiety, a tendency toward depression, or a multitude of other issues. Nevertheless, these factors need not keep us from maximizing our mental and psychological health.

Just as it is important to recognize your strengths it is important to be aware of your weaknesses. That's where acknowledging and confronting your demons come into play. Your demons are a signal that you are not dealing with some critical mental issue and, like physical pain they are telling you that action needs to be taken.

A cautionary note: demons are incredibly resilient, often lasting a lifetime. But they can be tamed. You can make enormous improvement in reducing their harmful effect. And you can learn how to fight them when they stick their ugly heads up. You can keep them at bay.

A major portion of this book emphasizes actions you can take to expand your strengths. Demons move your attention to your inner fears and weakness. They are the tip of the iceberg of inner doubt, representing deep concerns that hold you back from living life to its fullest. It is worth your time to confront those concerns. Don't let the demons win.

CHAPTER 37

Let Love In

IN MY YEARS as a therapist I have often come upon people who have difficulty accepting love. It's an astonishing observation, because we all believe the desire to be loved is universal. From our early years the hunger to be cared for and cherished appears natural. We are told to "love thy neighbor as thyself" as if loving one's self is standard and automatic. So it comes as a surprise that there are those who, in numerous ways, resist accepting the love of others.

In our infancy we are usually loved for "just being." We don't have to earn it. But, if, as we get older, our home life is filled with hostility and criticism, we learn self-protection mechanisms that temporarily shield us from hurt. Unfortunately these patterns can be over-learned and carried into adulthood, where they can be very damaging.

The inability to accept other's love from others is indeed an obstacle to happiness. It deprives a person of nourishment for confidence, self-esteem and respect, all contributors to feelings of well being. It interferes with reciprocal love, a source of much happiness.

A classic example was evident in a patient I treated many years ago. This young woman had come out of a very harsh and critical upbringing and was burdened with extremely poor self-esteem. Attempts to compliment her were adamantly resisted by her diminishing the appreciation — "Oh, anyone could have done that." — or other more self-deprecating statements. Interestingly, the one area where she felt comfortable was working with very young children — a population that couldn't offer criticism and where she felt safe. It was obvious that she felt unlovable.

Why would anyone not take in love? Actually there are many reasons. You may see them as irrational, but they nevertheless have merit in the eyes of those who have difficulty accepting love. Perhaps the most common reason is simply that the person does not feel worthy. Their self-perception has become so withered it doesn't make sense to them that anyone could love them.

Others may fear that if they take in the love, it may then be taken away — an experience so painful that they don't want to risk it again. Thus they create what some experts call a "broken receiver" — the inability to accept love due to devaluing praise or assuming the other person is insincere or other reasons of resistance. The psychological armor that was created initially to keep out the bad is now keeping out the good as well.

The inability to receive love is often very perplexing to the person's partner, for he or she may sincerely love their mate but find their efforts at sharing that feeling ineffective. In some cases they eventually give up, thus confirming, in the eyes of the "broken receiver" that he or she is really unlovable.

So what happened to this young woman? First of all let me share her treatment. She was admitted to the hospital in our chronic pain program for a period of three weeks with a primary diagnosis of intense and unrelenting headaches. It was clear to our team that her pain was significantly caused by severe muscle tension that in turn was created by her psychological issues. By group consensus we inundated her with praise — but not just general adulation. We listened carefully and sincerely to her history and discovered that she had been given awards for her writing abilities and had numerous other features that we could attend to.

We abundantly praised these and her progress in our program. We worked specifically to teach the benefits of allowing love and affection to be accepted and the harm done by denying its entrance. We were limited by circumstances to only three weeks of treatment so I cannot tell you that she was "cured." However, the change in her personality and the diminishing intensity of her headaches were substantial enough to tell us that we were on the right path.

Most people do not have a "broken receiver" as powerful as hers. For those who do, I recommend professional help. Such patterns can be tenacious and are unlikely to be altered by a few pep talks.

This story is not just for those who feel inadequate, lonely and unable to accept love, it is a message for all of us. We have all experienced a lifetime of being told to love and care for others. But loving others is not enough. It is critically important that we are *receptive* to love as well. When it is offered the person is giving us a gift. We should not deny the giver the pleasure of giving, and we should nourish our well being by accepting it.

Scour your personal landscape. Note the areas in which you can take quiet pride. Be sensitive to your strengths, talents and accomplishments. Allow these and the affection given to you to be fully absorbed. These are not to be denied. To be loved is one of the miracles of life. Don't waste it.

CHAPTER 38

You've Already Got An "A"

CLIENTS ARE OFTEN anxious the first time they see a therapist. Many have never seen a mental health professional and are nervous. It's understandable. To open up personal issues to a stranger can be frightening. To share perceived failings is to make oneself vulnerable — one of the reasons men are less likely than women to engage in therapy.

Anticipation, expectations and fear are the fuel of anxiety. We all live lives in which we are evaluated. From the everyday experience of what to wear to measures of job performance, we are sensitive to what others are thinking. Of course, for the insecure, even more so.

In an ideal world, receiving feedback should be seen as an opportunity to improve. But reality is different from the ideal. In the real world feedback goes through our personal filter, and we examine whether the evaluator is trustworthy, fair, and looking out for our interest, as well as a myriad of similar concerns. Such considerations put us on guard.

In establishing new therapeutic relationships I conscientiously attempt to reduce this initial worry over my evaluation. I know that, when anxieties are allayed, sessions are more comfortable and productive. My typical approach is to give assurances and also to lessen the evaluation component by addressing the anxiety. "It's not a problem. You've already got an A," is a comment my clients often hear.

I once employed this approach at the beginning of a senior level class I taught in college. The circumstances were special, but the results are worth noting. The class on behavior modification techniques was limited to those who already had knowledge of the subject and had passed an entrance exam. So, in effect, they had been evaluated already. But still, each student had natural concerns about his grade. On the first day of class I assured everyone that they would get an A. I also gave them the questions for their final exam. Again assuring them that no matter how they performed on tests, they were guaranteed an A. As classes go, the results were marvelous.

Contrary to what many would predict, attendance was perfect. Class participation was high and deeply engaged. Students expanded beyond the class content. They engaged with each other outside of class to share their thoughts. And they all got A's.

I don't assume that giving A's is a panacea to the many challenges of teaching or is appropriate in most college courses. But I do recommend addressing the anxiety many have in new situations by giving assurances. I am convinced that putting someone at ease is a pathway to opening doors. Perhaps not a great insight, you might say, but one that is often forgotten.

Even more important than directing this approach to others is to direct it towards yourself, a very difficult task. Notice for a moment, the many, many stories you've heard of great insights emerging in dreams. It is very likely that such creative thoughts occur, in part, because of the removal of a limiting censor, leaving the mind open to problem solve and wander unfettered into new territory. It is the removal of criticism that is crucial to the process. During these moments the mind is at ease.

In relationships, it is acceptance that fosters growth. In relationships it is trust that encourages deep bonding. When you give an A to someone you love, you open up marvelous opportunities. When you give it to yourself it's even better.

CHAPTER 39

It's Not Going on Your Permanent Record

I'VE OFTEN COUNSELED that, when worries become intense, one of the best problem solving techniques is to write out your concerns as specifically as possible. Next, spell out concrete actions that are under your control and those that aren't, such as other people's moods. It's advice that I follow. While it's often hard to get myself to write in this fashion, it's marvelously effective once done. For it typically moves me into action, and that, in and of itself, is a significant stress reliever.

But life is more than dealing with major problems. There are the little errors, failures, insults and aggravations of life. How does one prevent these annoyances from building up into a funk?

To me a critical approach is to deal with the small issues immediately, before they become bothersome. Preventing the hurt or feelings of failure when they are little, goes a long way toward maintaining a good mood. In the long run, it's almost like preventing crime by making sure that the streets are well lit and clean — actions that seem to deter more destructive results later on.

I find that the internal language people use plays a significant role in deciding whether the errors, failures, insults and aggravations grow or are pretty much stopped in their tracks. A few days ago a friend shared one of his little gems that I immediately promised to place in my mental first aid kit. After I made an embarrassing error, he reassured me with, "Don't worry, it's not going on your permanent record." I stood there surprised and smiling. Of course I could berate myself and ruminate over my error, but no, "It's not going on my permanent record." Wow! I can move on. It's no big thing in the large picture. Such were the sequential thoughts following his remark. I immediately felt better. I kept from getting frustrated with myself.

Mentally healthy people have what psychologists call self-compassion. Put another way, they are kind to themselves. The result of such self-compassion is that they, in turn, are kinder, more generous and tolerant of others — behaviors that provide enormous reciprocal rewards.

Self-compassion is a nice concept, warm and fuzzy. But how is it achieved? Certainly it is fortified with gratitude and quiet pride over personal strengths and accomplishments. But I suspect that it is largely maintained by keeping little human failings from expanding into significant self-doubt. When they return to the internal dialog immediately following a personal error, their dialog keeps the insults of life from growing into larger worries.

Self-compassion means forgiving yourself for making errors, and putting errors into the big picture perspective. The forgiveness is facilitated by your self-statements: "It's not going on your personal record" is one, but so is "Don't sweat the small stuff," and "It's not the end of the world" — all ways of managing life's irritations. I suspect if we were to analyze happy people we would find many have a catalog of constructive remarks that keep self-doubt at bay.

In protecting yourself from being overwhelmed by the slings and arrows of life I'm reminded of one of my favorite stories concerning Larry Doby, the first African-American to integrate the American League. Not as famous as Jackie Robinson in the National League, Larry Doby likewise endured tremendous racial abuse. He was asked after he retired whether he ever wished his skin were a different color. Without hesitation he replied, "I thank God that my skin is black. I just wish it were a little thicker."

Thick skin protecting us from life's tribulations is something we can all work on. It comes about from constructive thoughts immediately following a problem. I hope you have a lot of them at the ready. I was so pleased to recently add one more — "Don't worry. It's not going on your permanent record." Indeed I recommend that you make a list of your own and keep it handy.

Exercise
Don't Let the Bumps on Your Path Get You Off Track

Managing the everyday difficulties in life can be hard unless we have personal habits that help to smooth over the challenges. One means of doing that is to get in the habit of reminding ourselves of phrases that capture perspective.

See if you can come up with brief responses to frustrating situations such as the ones mentioned in this chapter:

1. It's not going on your personal record.

2. Don't sweat the small stuff

3. It's not the end of the world.

4.

5.

6.

CHAPTER 40

Keeping Worry at Bay

MARK TWAIN FAMOUSLY said, "Ninety-eight percent of what I worried about never happened." It appears to be an all too common trait to worry and fret about what might happen. Like Mark Twain, it's also true that we generally worry needlessly, or at least more than necessary. We project the worst and, in the process, often create more unhappiness than misfortune itself.

Worrying is a challenge, but there are some time-tested approaches that can soften the anxiety. Here are three of my favorites:

1. Gain perspective by going back in time to the most challenging moments in your life and recalling not just the problem that was faced but the deep-seated fear. Recall how you initially may have felt paralyzed, perhaps overwhelmed. And then remember how, in spite of some initial feelings of helplessness, you gathered strength and moved forward. Search for perseverance, intelligence, and diligence — whatever it was that carried you through the difficult time. These strengths are likely to still be available as a resource if given a chance to be resurrected. If any of these characteristics are part of your core image, they are likely to be very helpful in disempowering the worry.

2. Turn from oblique worry to creative problem solving. Worry is a form of pain and as such has a dominating effect. It tends to block out competing, often more rational, thoughts. Any

effort that interferes with the recycling of irrational thought will have benefit. Confronting the worry is valuable place to begin, but where? One approach is to simply consider the worst possible outcome. This oft-used technique is valuable because it transforms the oblique, vague anxiety into a concrete possibility, thereby making it more susceptible to problem solving.

Viewing the worst possible scenario immediately raises the question of whether you can survive the disaster, and more often than not the answer is yes. Yes, you've been poor, alone, sick — whatever — before. You got through it before and you can get through it again if it happens. It wasn't fun, but you did it. Reminding yourself that you've been there before and have survived takes the wind out of 'worry's sail most of the time.

3. Attend to your internal dialogue. This is a distinction that separates those who deal effectively with life's anxieties and those that don't. Happier people tend to use an internal dialog that differs from the worrier. You hear it in their little self-statements: "I've been down before and I pulled myself out. I'll do it again." "I remember feeling so depressed I didn't want to leave the house." These statements recognize that failure is a part of a normal life. Those who fail to manage their difficulties tend to focus on the present problem, failing to put their problems in perspective. Those who do manage their worries are more likely to be in tune with, "This too will pass."

Happiness takes smarts — the intelligence to incorporate little strategies that prevent sadness and anxiety from getting the upper hand. Gaining perspective is one such strategy, moving from oblique worry to concrete problem solving is another, and paying attention to your internal dialog a third — three approaches that can keep excessive worry at bay.

Mark Twain was right. The overwhelming percentage of our worries never come to pass. Being prepared is a good way to manage them when they do appear.

Exercise
Keep Worries at Bay While You Move Forward

Write out a particularly bothersome worry in the space below.

1. Gain perspective by remembering a period in your life when you had a worry similar to your current concern.

    a. Write out how you felt emotionally at the time.

    b. What personal strengths did you use to get through the difficulty?

2. Turn from oblique worry to creative problem solving.

    a. Consider the worse possible outcome that could result if your worry came true.

    b. Could you survive such an outcome? If the answer is yes, write out the steps you would need to take to survive.

3. Attend to your internal dialogue.

    a. Remind yourself that "This too will pass" or any other phrase that gives you perspective. Write out a similar statement that works for you.

CHAPTER 41

Rules: More important than you realize

WHEN YOU WERE a child in school, you had rules to follow: no gum chewing in class, no copying from your neighbor. At home you were not allowed to hit, use foul language or throw food. As an adult you might feel that you have few rules — one of the privileges of being an adult. After all, if you want to eat a pint of ice cream, there's no one to stop you. But a closer look reveals that you do have rules — self-imposed rules. And the rules you establish for your life are critical to your well being.

For example, in determining the quality of a marriage here's a rule that is strikingly important: no name-calling. Sounds straight out of childhood, doesn't it? According to John Gottman, psychologist and author of *The Seven Principles For Making Marriage Work*, breaking or not having this rule is one the most harmful things a spouse can do.[21] Why? Because negative names and labels leave emotional scars. They create lasting memories. They damage trust, an element at the heart of any good relationship. Breaking this rule brings natural negative consequences.

No name-calling is just one of dozens of rules you might make for yourself. Most people don't think about them unless pushed. Rules are said to oneself so often they became automatic and are unspoken. Some can determine both our character and our well being, others

---

21 Gottman, H. and Silver, N., *The Seven Principles for Making Marriage Work*, Three Rivers Press, New York, NY, 1999.

are minor. A minor rule might be, "I don't honk at other drivers." A favorite of mine from a near-vegetarian is, "I don't eat anything that can look me directly in the eyes," thereby allowing chicken and fish to be consumed since their eyes are on the sides of their heads. Technically debatable, but it works for him.

A man who views himself as a gentleman might have a rule that he never swears in public or in front of women. Another might have rules about his sexual behavior or how he dresses. We may believe that our rules are untouchable, never to be altered. Some of us are proud of our rules. You may have heard of the two centenarians philosophizing about their longevity and really speaking about personal rules. One says that she never smoked or drank a day in her life. The other, just as proudly, professes that his longevity is a result of a stiff drink and a good cigar every day.

Some rules may be controversial to others but work for the individual. A couple I knew had an arrangement — a rule — that most couples would find unacceptable. Their rule allowed the husband to have affairs while on his many business trips but never to stray at home. Nor was he ever allowed to discuss his trysts. By all external signs the couple had a deep loving relationship. When the wife suffered a prolonged battle with cancer at the end of her life, he was there every moment, lovingly giving his all.

Most rules are less controversial but can still cause enormous distress. Here are examples taken from clients. Each one was considered inviolate and each created emotional chaos. "I must have two million dollars in order to be secure." "I must love my children no matter what." "My house must always be immaculate." "I must meet my father's standards in order to be loveable." Each one of these self-imposed rules was an underlying cause of great distress for the individual or their spouse and ultimately brought them to therapy. You may find some of them reasonable, yet when followed obsessively can cause havoc.

Modifying a rule is difficult. We can all find evidence that confirms our rules even when the rules do not serve us well. It's worthwhile to identify your rules and examine them. Consider whether any of them diminish the quality of your life today. Rules have the power to enhance or damage a life. Take them seriously and be sure that yours enhance your well being.

Exercise

Know Your Own Rules as You Travel Along

Discovering your own rules may be difficult. Many of our rules are so automatic that we are not immediately aware that they exist. It's useful, however, to do a little searching to clarify your rules. Examine those behaviors about which you feel very strong, such as loyalty, honesty, hard work, fidelity, foul language, fairness, alcohol, drugs, dietary habits and cleanliness. After giving each of these some thought you may come up with additional areas not listed. Write down at least four rules that you feel are critical to who you are:

1.

2.

3.

4.

Once you've written down your rules, consider if the rule serves you well, were appropriate at one time in your life, but not presently, and have outlived their usefulness.

CHAPTER 42

The High Cost of Always Being Right

LET'S CONSIDER JIMMY, a fictitious character who is a composite of spouses I've heard described in my work. He believes he is ALWAYS right, but unbeknownst to him, his marriage is paying a high price. Usually the offending person is a husband, but occasionally a wife. Jimmy's spouse comes to me and reports that her opinion is rarely requested and, if given, is usually ignored or overridden.

When one person in a marriage believes he is always right, the relationship suffers. Such behavior may have worked in the Victorian age with male supremacy the order of the day, but modern marriages, or at least successful ones, usually demand a more respectful and egalitarian union.

Spouses requesting my help generally arrive with feelings of frustration, depression and anxiety. They are unhappy. They feel unfulfilled and underappreciated. There is a great deal of tension in their homes. They often feel as if they are walking on eggshells, afraid that they will be criticized at any moment.

When one party believes that his way is the correct way to the point of stifling opposition or even discussion, there is likely to be difficulty. Or still worse, those like Jimmy may demand that others *absolutely* adhere to his standards. Big trouble!

It is wonderful to be right. It feels good. It's gratifying. It's good for your ego. But it's also dangerous. Dangerous in the sense that it can be addictive to believe that your opinion is always better and your judgment should prevail. However, the temporary advantage of feeling superior and getting your way is offset by long-term damage to the relationship and the spouse. Such dominance strangles emotions. It hampers problem solving. It promotes anger and fosters resentment.

It is interesting to hear that these clients love their partners, often very deeply. I ask them to tell me their spouse's positive characteristics and they list many. The offending partner is not a bad person, they say. But their spouse has fallen into a pattern that is harmful to the relationship.

My clients are sometime complicit in maintaining this pattern. They may be unassertive and unwilling to stand up for their needs. They may harbor feelings of inferiority that make it easier for the pattern to continue. Invariably I ask to meet with the spouse who is always right. Of course, that may not be Jimmy's self-perception. If Jimmy is unwilling to meet, we work on improving what the client can control, such as communication, assertiveness and self-esteem.

It's always easier to improve relationships when both partners participate and work toward a mutually agreed upon goal. In many therapeutic situations that ideal situation is not possible. Then it is necessary to manage what you can control. A difficult circumstance, but one worth pursuing.

Studies by social scientists clearly show that problem solving is much more productive when done by more than a single mind. Working together, people are more creative and effective in achieving their goal. They learn to empathize and understand each other at a deeper level. This often takes more time and effort.

To the person who always gets his way, it may feel that the problem is finished faster and better when he or she makes the decision. It is less messy in the short run. But in the long run the person who suffers the indignity of having their opinion discounted can experience severe consequences, often affecting their feelings for their spouse. Being right all or most of the time is a classic case of winning the battle and losing the war — or the marriage in this case.

CHAPTER 43

Old Messages

My wife, Gail, recently had a bad episode in the kitchen and called me to come to the rescue. She was making a pecan pie, had placed it on a cookie sheet that didn't quite fit our oven and had spilled it on the floor — quite a mess. Now Gail is a very strong, independent and self-assured woman who, on this occasion, suffered a temporary loss of confidence.

I should note that I do almost all the cooking in our house and Gail, as a general rule, does not like to cook. I, on the other hand, love to cook but am a miserable soul when it comes to fixing things around the house. When I attempt to repair anything mechanical, it often turns into a disaster, and Gail is the one to the rescue. On those occasions, it is not only self-doubt that comes to mind, but foul words to my mouth along with an increase in blood pressure.

Why these reactions? As Gail wailed during her pie disaster, "Every woman in the world can make a pie except me!" Remember this is coming from an accomplished MBA who handles many challenging projects comfortably. And the implicit message somewhere in the back of my mind when I am facing the overflowing toilet — "What kind of idiot male can't do a simple thing like fix a toilet?"

To me these reactions are the result of cultural sex-role training that has been imbedded in our psyche. Somewhere in Gail's mind, whether she would openly recognize or admit it, is the message, "I'm a woman. I should be able to cook well." And comparably, my brain is pulsating with a message that argues, "You're a man. You should be able to repair things."

Interestingly, our respective cross-sex-role abilities have carried us far. Gail receives praise for her mechanical skills, and I am often the recipient of admiration for my culinary talents. But that doesn't stop each of us from replaying those silly messages from our childhoods.

Of course, everyone can cite many current examples of cross-sex-role exceptions (e.g., male nurses and female pilots) but the dominant cultural message is still macho and Eros. Just look in toy stores or at magazines racks to see if sex-role typing is a thing of the past. No, the old messages are still receiving a great deal of modern repetition. So we continue — bright, capable adults — self-flagellating with unwarranted criticism.

You might be interested to know that today's teen-agers continue to be influenced by the same messages we received when we were children. How can that be, you might argue. After all, don't today's youth know about the feminist movement and gender equality? Well, yes — sort of. It turns out that high school boys score high on sensitivity to feminine issues, but at the same time, they also score extremely high on macho measures. Apparently the boys know the right thing to say regarding female issues but simultaneously hold very high traditional male attitudes, thus having self-denigrating thoughts if they act too feminine. Similar inconsistencies hold for the girls as well.

I've highlighted some gender role self-messages, but I could easily cite non-gender role messages that are instrumental in causing angst. Here are a few messages that have created emotional problems for many of my clients: "I need to be perfect," "My home should always be neat," "I should never offend anyone with what I say," "It's awful if I am ever late," and "I must never get angry."

These old self-critical messages are likely well embedded. Consequently, removing these often outdated and counterproductive messages can be a challenge, but it is a battle worth fighting. Even your parents would probably agree that they can be carried too far.

You might want to write down some of your old messages. They could be getting in the way as you travel on your path to happiness.

Overview of Section 6

Cherish Your Relationships

IN STEPHEN COVEY's very influential book, *The 7 Habits of Highly Effective People*, the author highlights the importance of prioritizing our goals and behaviors, paying attention to those areas that we most cherish. Family and relationships tend to be at the top of that list. Yet most of us are more likely to devote the majority of our attention to non-essentials such as "screen time." Getting your priorities in order and acting upon them is a major decision in creating your path to well being and happiness.

The science of positive psychology clearly shows that those who have a larger network of family and friends, not only tend to live happier lives, they also tend to live longer lives. When relationships are deep and plentiful, the effects are magnified.

Few will argue against the value of deep relationships. The problem comes not in believing that relationships are important, but in putting this knowledge into practice. We need not berate ourselves for lapses but understand that regular reminders to return to what most of us cherish is a wise habit to maintain.

CHAPTER 44

Stories

Last night was delightful — a spontaneous dinner party with some new friends. Besides liking everyone, I got to thinking about why it was such an exceptional evening. The answer was simple: we all shared stories, interesting and funny.

At one point I had the urge to tell a story, an amusing tale involving an unexpected invitation to dinner, hot dogs and beans, and pet white rats running loose. As I waited my turn, I noticed that I had a "hunger" to speak, to participate and share and, if I didn't, I'd be missing out. There's obviously a pleasure in sharing stories — smiling, laughing, and learning more about each other. Over my years of teaching I've observed that students believe a class is better when they have participated. From the first time humans sat around a fire, it seems that there has been a need to share and, when stories can't be told, we can have an empty feeling.

Not all sharing is positive. Storytelling can be spoiled by people who don't listen, those who converse only to promote themselves or who have to always be right and, sadly, by some who don't have any stories to tell. But excluding those issues, storytelling is an elixir and one I thoroughly enjoy.

Stories bond us to each other. What a delight it is to see long-time friends and jump into the pool of mutual stories. Just as our bodies become conditioned to fearful situations, we also have physical changes when reminded of the pleasant experiences of life. The pleasure center of our brain lights up; it feels as if the heart literally skips a beat with pleasure. People with a greater network of friends live longer. There's a well-documented body of evidence attesting to this. It's not simply that we have friends to share our distress and troubles, it's also because we can share our stories of glee.

Storytelling can heal as well. This seemed to be true for many chronic pain patients. Such patients frequently believe that they are alone with an unknown diagnosis. In such an atmosphere, early sessions with groups of chronic pain patients bring a palatable sense of relief as they share their circumstances and ambiguous diagnoses. They are sharing similar stories and thereby reducing their sense of being alone and feeling hopeless. Knowing that you have a difficult issue is a challenge but less so when shared with others. Similarly, it turns out that while it's hard to be poor, it's somewhat easier surrounded by others who are struggling, rather than to be poor around those who are wealthy. Sharing woes, not done to excess, makes life just a bit easier.

Truth be told, psychotherapy is, in large part, helping people revise their inner story. Of course each patient comes with a troubling issue, but that problem is typically told in the context of a story. Listening carefully to the patient's narrative reveals their self-identity, their view of the world and the manner in which they interact. Arguing against their viewpoint is useless, but reflecting it back and providing alternatives can be constructive. In the best of circumstances patients progress through therapy learning a different story about their issue and often about themselves.

Stories are one reason why we want to be with others — they show our common love. Many years ago I gathered five sets of my aunts and uncles together for a brief video taping and separately asked each couple the simple question, "How did you meet?" Nervous in front of a camera at the outset, each couple broke into smiles and often competed with each other to tell their story. It was as if a door had been opened and together they walked back into a memory, smiling and laughing as the other spoke and jumping in to add a detail to their shared pictures — a joyous experience. It should be noted that these were long, mostly successful marriages. Sharing common stories helped them to be so.

Compare this positive experience to a very different story detailed in John Gottman's book, *The Seven Principles for Making Marriage Work*. Gottman, a leader in his field of research on marital relationships, cites shared memories as one of the foundation stones of a successful marriage. In one poignant example, a husband was unable to remember where the couple had gone on their honeymoon or anything about the event, a significant indicator that the marriage was in serious trouble. Don't despair if you're unable to remember every detail, but if pleasant, shared memories are absent or few, it speaks poorly of your relationship. Relationships are critical to your well being, and stories are cement that helps hold them together.

Now remember that story about the hot dogs and beans and pet white rats? Well, the thing is it was at a job interview and . . .

CHAPTER 45

Your Own Little Study

THE WORLD OF positive psychology has unleashed an avalanche of surveys and studies examining the happiest people in the world. To me, the results are intriguing, but sometimes contradictory. For example, authoritarian countries tend to have very low levels of happiness, but one of the happiest countries turns out to be the very authoritarian Singapore, a stunning exception.

There are other surprising findings as well; the senior population is, on the whole, happy. Disabled people are happier than most people would expect and, while having more money makes the very poor happier, there is an upper limit where additional income appears to have little additional happiness benefit.

I find these surveys and studies gripping because I am immersed in the study of well being, but I wonder if most people couldn't learn a great deal just by systematically examining the people they know.

When I look around at my friends and relatives, there definitely are those who seem to generally be very, very happy. And likewise, there are others who are miserable. Interestingly, the unhappy ones are more rare. In our society, Gallup and other pollsters report that roughly 80% of the population professes to be happy most of the time, and within that group a smaller percentage, roughly 33%, are very happy. That leaves only 20% who are unhappy or very unhappy.

So as you look around, you might have a more difficult time coming up with the unhappy ones. But I believe the effort is worthwhile. Here's what I'm suggesting. Think of the two happiest people that you know, people that you know well enough to describe their habits, life-style and attitudes. Now think of two others that are unhappy. As I say, you may have a harder time listing unhappy people, but I bet at least one will quickly come to mind, and with a little more mental searching you may be able to come up with a second. Then detail as much as you can about each of your four people. Write out your observations with particular attention to thinking styles and habits. The exercise, by the way, is likely to be especially enlightening if done in partnership with a spouse or a very close friend.

I did find differences between my two groups. My unhappy people tend to be more moody and much more distrustful of others and institutions. The other thing that jumped out of my very unscientific and extremely limited sample was the frequent blaming of others by my two unhappy acquaintances.

My happy people, on the other hand, are more upbeat, optimistic, more likely to find the silver lining in every cloud and certainly appreciative of their good fortune.

But do your own little study. See if you can find distinguishing habits and attitudes that separate those who are happy and unhappy. We tend to associate with people who share our general economic, racial and even political background, so the differences we are likely to observe are those of personality and attitude. That turns out to be fortunate. For it is personality and attitude that are most under our control and therefore the difference where we can gain the most.

To some extant my observations confirmed my suspicions as to what is important. They also made me think about what lessons I can learn and what I need to do in order to maximize my own happiness. It took me about forty minutes to write it out. It made me think. It was worth the effort.

Exercise

Choose Your Travel Companions Carefully

1. Do a little mental survey of your friends rating them as mostly happy or unhappy.

2. Choose two of the most happy and unhappy out of each group.

3. As best you can, speculate on their most prominent mental approach to managing difficult situation, such as "This too shall pass," or "Why do bad things always happen to me." Write them out.

CHAPTER 46

Communicating Love

AT THE TIME of this writing, the book *Five Love Languages: How to communicate love in a way a spouse will understand* by Gary Chapman has been on the New York Times Love and Relationship best sellers list an unprecedented 285 weeks — that's 5 plus years. What is it that makes this self-help book, first published in 1992, so incredibly popular and enduring?

The fact that it is clearly written and the concept easy to understand is crucial, but most importantly, Chapman has hit upon a psychological truth: we often talk past one another in our conversations, especially with those people whom we love. As a result good people and decent relationships often flounder.

But before I expand on the heart of the *Five Love Languages*, let's take a second to explore the problem Chapman is addressing.

To begin with, romantic love is a form of insanity. There, I said it! It's a fairy tale and it's crazy — a wonderful crazy to be sure, a feeling like no other, full of joy and ecstasy. The crazy label is not just hype. Recent MRI studies consistently show that the same areas of the brain that evidence insanity also "light up" during the love experience. I am not arguing against this "insanity," merely pointing out that from a scientific standpoint passionate love is a highly unusual state.

The difficulty begins when the insanity subsides and the work of marriage, or any long-term relationship, begins. To illustrate: Researchers followed 1,761 couples who married and stayed married over a 15-year period. The results were strong and clear. Newlyweds enjoyed very high levels of happiness that lasted on average about two years, followed by a decline to levels prior to their "insanity." This finding, published in 2003, has been confirmed by several more recent studies.

A personal take on the above research is illustrated in what a psychologist friend called the "French fry phenomenon." His vision was that of a man looking adoringly across a restaurant table watching the love of his life daintily eat a French fry, thinking that no other creature on earth can so delicately place a French fry into her month. To the lover, the action is breathtaking. Advance two years, and the same action has lost its magic. Now, as he views the same scene, it seems that her eating is ordinary, perhaps overly slow and maybe even gross. Even more likely, he can hardly remember that he ever reveled in such fantasy.

Of course, when we are in the midst of passionate love we are hypersensitive to the positive features of our lover and blind to their lesser qualities. As time passes we move on to what experts call compassionate love, a less impassioned combination of affection and connection. The reason this happens is that humans are disposed to "hedonic adaptation" — the innate tendency to become habituated to life's pleasures. Stated a bit differently, we are thrilled by positive experiences but, over time, begin to take them for granted.

So how does this relate to the *Five Love Languages* book? Chapman argues that once we morph beyond the passionate love stage, we tend to return to our more well established patterns of communicating love. He persuasively argues that we are likely to *give* love in the manner that we have learned to *receive* it during our formative years. In other words, we give what we want to receive. Sounds fine until we realize that our individual version of love may be quite different than that of our partner.

To take a classic example: a man may believe that giving his wife a life of economic security is his highest form of love, while the wife may believe that spending quality time with her mate is the best expression of love. If the husband obsessively pursues work while the wife's expects quality time together, eventually there will be a problem. And that is what often happens. Couples very often don't *hear* the love that is being expressed, and don't *give* the love they don't know is wanted.

What makes the Chapman book so compelling is that it helps husband and wife examine how they would like to receive love. In doing so a conversation can ensue to bring the discrepancies between what is given as love and what is received as love into balance.

The evolution from passionate to compassionate love is not to be discounted as something less — it is simply different and wonderful in its own right. But, for compassionate love to grow, communication is necessary — something nicely laid out in Gary Chapman's book. There is a reason it's been on the best sellers list for so long.

CHAPTER 47

Wow! How Exciting; Tell Me the Details

I RECENTLY CAME across an exciting exercise that I'm bubbling to tell you about. It was touted in Martin Seligman's newest book, *Flourish*. It's a bit complicated to explain, but if practiced, the results are likely to be wonderful. Plus it's just plain fun.

The neat thing about this exercise is that it's not simply a remedy for a problem, but also an enhancement for those of us who are getting along pretty well. You might remember that the burgeoning field of Positive Psychology is not about remedying a deficit but building on to what may already be good. And that especially applies to relationships, the focus of this particular exercise.

According to researchers, there are four different response styles that people offer when reacting to hearing positive news. Think "I received a promotion" or "My biopsy was benign" or something more common like "I had a great day." The responses to good news typically fall into four categories: Active and constructive, passive and constructive, active and destructive and passive and destructive. The response styles become very clear when we lay them out.

Active/Constructive	Active/Destructive
Passive/Constructive	Passive/Destructive

Let's take the one style that is fabulously beneficial to a relationship — active and constructive. Let's say that you hear, "I just learned that the project I've been working on has been accepted." An active and constructive response might go like this: "That's wonderful!" said with excitement and energy. "I'm so proud of you. I knew you could do it. You've got such determination. When did you hear? Give me all the details." The nonverbals are similarly enthusiastic, with genuine smiling, eye contact, laughing and touching.

You may believe that you already respond with an active and constructive response, but let's contrast that with the other categories that happen all too often. A passive and constructive response might include positive things such as "That's good news" or "That's nice, dear," but said with a flat demeanor. The less than enthusiastic response creates a mismatch between the excitement felt in the speaker's accomplishment and the passive response. This discrepancy is likely to feel like a letdown. It's the sharing in the emotional high that connects people and it is missing in this style.

The third, and also sadly depleting reply, is the active and destructive response. Here the responder takes a pessimistic view, focusing on the negative. An active and destructive response might be, "Oh, I guess that means you're going to be given another project now" or "You know that they never really appreciate what a hard worker you are." Again, you can easily imagine how such a response might take the wind out of your sail — hardly a way to cement a relationship.

The fourth style is perhaps the most destructive. The researchers title this reply, passive and destructive. Hearing an excited, "My project has been accepted" is met with "What's for dinner" with no eye contact or any other acknowledgement. You can only imagine how deflating and punishing such a response would feel.

Let's go back for a moment to detail why the active and constructive style is so beneficial and worth cultivating. When someone tells you good news, they are expressing what they value, as well as sharing where they have put their time and energy. Expressing your own excitement in response doesn't simply acknowledge the news, it says you value them and believe in them — extraordinarily important messages in a relationship.

Exercise

Keeping Your Companions Close

Take the next week to elevate a relationship to a level that is dynamically <u>active</u> and <u>constructive</u>.

Be on the lookout for things that your spouse, partner, friend say that reveal their sense of accomplishment and pride. Jump on those remarks with mutual excitement, in some cases, even exceeding theirs.

Record your effort and note the response you receive to your effort:

Write down the name of your friend or partner/spouse:

Their news:

Your spoken response to their news:

I've often written that happiness takes work and that a critical pillar to happiness and well being is strong relationships. Well, here's the work. No matter how often you believe that you already practice healthy replies to good news, take the next week to elevate them to a level that is dynamically <u>active</u> and <u>constructive</u>. I confidently predict that your excitement to good news will be abundantly repaid.

CHAPTER 48

Doing Friends a Favor – What an Opportunity

Friends recently called with what they referred to as an emergency request. Certainly not a life-threatening situation, but a needed favor to avoid a major inconvenience. Their ride to the airport had fallen through just as they were about to walk out the door, and they wondered if I could be their Good Samaritan and immediately drive them.

No problem, sure, of course, you're my friends. But what seemed like a bit of altruism was much more. We're all aware that friends do things for one another, and are the people that we hope will be there in times of need. But, friends being friends, we tend not to request favors very often, lest we be annoying or worse. Therein lies a problem. We simply don't get that many opportunities to provide acts of kindness to the very people we treasure and others that we like. So I say, when the opportunity to give or receive arises, jump at it.

As so often expressed in these pages, friends and friendships cannot be overvalued. They are a pillar of good mental health and happiness, a cornerstone of physical health and longevity. Close relationships with intimate sharing and vulnerability can be an extraordinary balm to hurt and grieving.

In our very individualistic society the need to appear independent and self-sufficient is great. As a result we are often reluctant to avail ourselves of assistance from others. "Oh no, I can manage," is a frequent refrain. The fear of infringing or inconveniencing enters our thought process. It's a natural but unfortunate pattern, for it interferes with the bonding between friends. It is in just such a situation where gentle insistence to help can be very positive. Pushing the door open to doing a favor has few downsides, unless you're pushing too hard.

Many years ago a close friend was in a difficult situation that was augmented by fear of what might happen in the future. I was in a position to help the person with little hardship to myself. Decades have passed and I doubt if the person even remembers the transaction in the same manner that I do. Nevertheless, my action was simple but the consequences *to me* were significant. At the time I jumped at the chance to make a difference in this person's life and have never regretted it. As it turned out, my actions did cause me some difficulty. But that was a trade I made at the time, and the story I can tell myself is worth the cost. That is just one of the additional benefits of stepping up when the opportunity arises.

What we say in our personal appraisal and self-talk is not a minor item. As a matter of fact, it is crucial to our well being. The more stories we have that support a sense of self respect and love, the better off we are. Being there for friends is a building block of maturity. And interestingly, such action is a multiplier. It yields reciprocal kindnesses and a feeling of connection. It also promotes a feeling of well being that allows us to increase kindness to those around us.

The kindest gift we can give to others is to build happiness within ourselves. One of the most straightforward building blocks to that happiness is the give-and-take generosity we share with others around us. Truly a win-win situation.

CHAPTER 49

The Hidden Cost of Silence

PSYCHOLOGICAL RESEARCH CLEARLY shows that not being able to express a full range of your emotions is detrimental to well being. One psychologist goes so far as to claim that 80% of men suffer from this deficiency.

I don't know if 80% is accurate but, whatever the number, I can categorically state that withholding emotions is harmful. A psychologist at the University of Texas, James Pennebaker, has spent his professional life examining this proposition and his research is compelling.[22]

Dr. Pennebaker shows that a wide variety of traumas can leave lasting emotional scars, but those victims who hide their personal pain tend to fare much worse. Interestingly, the damage is not confined to psychological adjustment but affects physical health as well. In a survey of 200 respondents who had experienced at least one childhood trauma, the 65 who kept their histories secret had a higher incidence of a broad range of health problems such as cancer, high blood pressure, headaches and ulcers. The results of this study link the hidden price of silence with harmful effects not only upon the body's immune system, but also on more general physical and psychological health.

---

22 Pennebaker, J. *Opening Up: The Healing Power of Expressing Emotions*, The Guilford Press, New NY, 1997.

There is now a large body of evidence that states that, if people talk about their problems, their health improves and, conversely, not talking about important emotional events is a health risk. Organizations that focus on drug and alcohol abuse, eating disorders, compulsive gambling, divorce, and victimization from a wide range of abuse are valuable and effective, in part, because they facilitate talking and sharing.

Not all talking and sharing is valuable, however, nor does everyone with a problem wish to attend a meeting for every problem in his or her life. For most people, this is where friends come into the picture — good friends. Research even shows that the more friends you have, the healthier you are. More important, however, is the degree to which you talk to your friends about issues that trouble you.

This last point is critical. The benefit of having many friends disappears in terms of your health, if you have had a trauma and have not spoken about it with your friends. Merely having friends is not enough to protect you unless you use the opportunity to share your upset with them.

For those who hide their emotional distress over a lifetime there is a consequence — most often with feelings of isolation and loneliness. This inner anguish is sometimes buried behind obsessive preoccupation with activities, such as work, that temporarily cover up the emotional pain. But the shame, embarrassment, regret and hurt remain.

In one of the more dramatic examples of the hidden price of silence, Dr. Pennebaker and his colleagues interviewed Holocaust survivors who had not spoken of their ordeal since arrival in the United States many decades earlier. So horrific was their experience that only 30% of those interviewed had ever spoken to anyone about it. "I've tried to forget about it" or "I didn't want to upset my children" were common reasons for their failure to share.

In a series of two-hour interviews that the researchers found immensely painful, Pennebaker reported that almost all of the

Holocaust survivors found the disclosures to have a beneficial effect on both themselves and their families. And in a one-year follow-up, researchers found that the survivors who were least likely to disclose with detail and openness were significantly more likely to see a physician for illness than those who had spoken openly.

What is it that causes the lack of self-disclosure to be harmful and the process of sharing to be beneficial? One much-supported hypothesis is simply that those who hide their distress ruminate over their upset. In addition, their internal stories tend to be incomplete and thus cause continuing pain. Sharing, on the other hand, allows community and perspective to enter into the story, while permitting some closure to their distress. Whether this interpretation is accurate or not, there is no question that there is a significant cost to silence and a compelling benefit to sharing your emotions with others.

CHAPTER 50

Well, You're Finally Not Eating Like a Pig

ONE OF THE important findings emerging from the field of positive psychology is that it takes at least five good acts to offset the damage created by one destructive one. So a minimum of five complements are needed to overcome the harm created by one insult. It turns out, however, that the simple act of giving a compliment is not so effortless after all.

You might think that everyone knows how to give a compliment. Such a notion came crashing to the floor on one occasion when I gave the "five to one" recipe to a casual acquaintance. Knowing that I was a psychologist, this fellow stopped me and asked my advice. As a general rule it's unwise to provide such, "on the run" pointers, but I succumbed and ill-advisedly gave this man a recommendation.

It seems that his adolescent daughter was disrespectful and unruly — from his vantage point, totally out of control. After listening to him detail her insolence, I encouraged him to begin to focus on whatever morsel of good behavior he could find, compliment it and observe any minute change. One week later he came back, somewhat disgruntled, complaining that my recommendation was worthless. Surprised at the failing of a usually highly successful approach, I asked for an example of what he had done.

"Well," he began, with much frustration, "I noticed that she was eating nicely and I told her, 'Well, you're finally not eating like a pig.'" Stifling a laugh, I asked whether he thought there was anything wrong with his compliment and immediately realized that he was oblivious to its derision. His relationship had deteriorated to the point where he was not only overly focused on his daughter's faults, but also insensitive to his own contribution to the situation.

Part of the problem, of course, is that we sometimes get out of the habit of complimenting. Big mistake. Compliments help to cement relationships — all relationships, both close and casual. They reward or reinforce those behaviors that please us and codify the gratefulness that we feel. They tell others that we value them and their behaviors.

Compliments are more powerful when we pay attention to what others are saying and especially to their motives and feelings. In doing so we give important attention to what is happening in their life and hence provide them with a feeling of worth.

Another consideration in skillful complimenting is sincerity. Compliments given casually simply don't have as much clout as those that are sincerely felt. So how is that achieved? A direct way is to put in the time to listen carefully, looking for perhaps the most powerful ingredients to a good compliment — evidence.

Telling someone that they "look nice" is a very nice compliment and one that is likely to have some impact. Telling that same person that they "always look nice" and then providing examples of clothing they have worn is a major step in magnifying the compliment. The more evidence the better.

There are many people who are somewhat immune to compliments, ironically most likely those with poor self-esteem, and thus the ones who could benefit the most. For such individuals compliments often roll off them like water off a duck's back. The compliment can only penetrate if it has some persuasive quality, and persuasion is more likely when accompanied by evidence.

It may sound a bit complicated to be sincere, attentive and evidence seeking. But such effort has astounding rewards, not just for the recipient but, for you as well. Giving compliments is one of those skills that rebounds many fold. You give the compliment, but you're likely to receive friendship and love in return — not a bad exchange at all.

Exercise

Compliment Often, and Well

You may believe that you already are very good at giving compliments. Good. All the more reason to test out your assumption while also observing the effect of consistently complimenting another person.

For the next 7 days give 5 compliments each day, without repeat, to a person of your choice. Make a check mark in the boxes below for each compliment given.

Day	Compliment 1	Compliment 2	Compliment 3	Compliment 4	Compliment 5
1					
2					
3					
4					
5					
6					
7					

Observe any changes in the person chosen. The reaction may be different on days 1 and 2 than on days 6 and 7.

CHAPTER 51

Playing Well in the Sandbox

"YOU NEVER PAY attention to me. You're just like your father — a cold fish." "Oh yeah, if you weren't such a blabbermouth, maybe I'd be able to get a word in edgewise."

This might be the opening salvo in a marital therapy session. Each side, often filled with venom, responding to each verbal assault with a counter of their own — like a grudge match, each hit filled with emotional baggage designed to do the utmost damage.

If left to its own momentum, this emotional intensity may continue unabated until one or the other explodes in disgust, turning to the therapist for support or relief. At home the same escalation often advances to a slammed door, sullen withdrawal or, in the worst case, physical violence.

The comparison between couples who "argue well" and those that don't is highly predictive of the quality of a marriage. Those relationships that engage in destructive exchanges have a low likelihood of success since many of their actions, such as name-calling and certainly physical abuse, leave long-term scars. Resentment, piled up like dried kindling, make future arguments burn hotter and retards healing. Mental recycling builds layers of blame and ironclad certainty makes reconciliation that much more difficult. The resulting hurt fuels distrust and fear, limiting closeness. Given such conditions it seems surprising that peace can ever be restored.

The techniques used by marital therapists to facilitate healing can be helpful in understanding how to build good relationships and avoid the problems in the first place. The goal, of course, is to learn to "play well in the sandbox" — a metaphor for getting along and even arguing well — something we try to teach our children at early age. We all have differences with those whom we care for, and it's smart to keep differences from degenerating into heated and destructive arguments.

One of the most effective styles that expert marital therapist John Gottman details is the use humor to interrupt an escalating argument. Such an approach requires both parties to deescalate once an agreed upon signal is expressed. Gottman cites one couple that abbreviates an argument when one or the other puts their tongue between their lips and blows hard making a silly noise. The Meta message here is that "Our argument is getting too heated. Let's cool it and get back to it when we're not so agitated." It may sound absurd and that particular gesture may not be the right one for you, but such a habit has saved many a marriage.

Marital therapists often require each party to patiently listen to the other's perception so closely that they can *summarize it to the first person's satisfaction*. Often in heated exchanges, each party is likely to be gearing up their response, not putting their energy into listening, but preparing to counter instead. Requiring listening, to the point that satisfies the other person, accomplishes two goals; it tells the other that their point of view is actually being heard and secondly it increases the likelihood that the viewpoint is understood not just at the surface, but reaching underlying feelings and motives as well.

A third technique used to keep each party on track is to disallow past history detours from sabotaging the problem solving efforts. "Oh yeah, you're a slob" doesn't help to resolve a financial dispute. Thus most therapists will regularly set a rule that participants must stick to the primary topic, and the therapist will interrupt to maintain on-track exchanges.

Of course this is just a sampling of techniques used by marriage therapists, and they are not magic. They sometimes take many, many, many hours of effort. Nevertheless the approaches can teach us something.

First, when arguments have continued and escalated to a damaging level, they are very difficult to resolve. The scars and hurt can be tremendously difficult to overcome in the future. Therefore, make every effort to interrupt an escalating argument before it gets out of hand.

Secondly, listen carefully not just to the other person's argument, but see if you can restate it to be sure you understand their feelings and motives.

Third, do your best to stay on topic. If a disagreement can be transformed into problem solving, you're on the right track.

Difference of opinions and arguments are a part of life. Those who know how to get along in spite of those differences are likely to smile a lot more often than those who don't.

CHAPTER 52

Sensitivity to Others' Feelings

THE PATH TO happiness and well being has some clear road signs: control what you can control, be grateful, exercise, and nurture your friendships. There are other factors, not so obvious, however, that deserve attention. One of the most critical is sensitivity to the feelings of others. Those who possess this quality are at a big advantage when it comes to relationship building.

Consider the observation that you can't tell the physician who graduated at the top of his or her classes from one near the bottom. There is some truth to this. Most patients are not drawn to doctors because of their academic rankings. More likely, they are drawn to doctors who put them at ease and are sensitive to their feelings. They return to that doctor's office again and again.

A physician colleague of mine was particularly sensitive to his patient's anxiety and used a clever technique to combat it. He had an elegant higher than normal chair in his office. If he noticed that a patient was uneasy, he would have them sit in it, reducing their anxiety. Far from being embarrassed, they would become relaxed and forthcoming. Picking up on my friend's example I once treated an anxious patient by sitting on the floor while my patient, initially fearful, became quite relaxed and loquacious.

Sensitivity and empathy go hand in hand. Both are gateways to connections with others, even by the simple act of recognition. The awareness of another person's sadness, depression, anxiety, anger, happiness, glee, etc. can be an enormous bridge to a conversation.

Here is an example of just such a situation. I once had an office on the same floor as a locked psychiatric ward and was on call if any problem occurred. One day a highly agitated psychiatric aid came running into my office exclaiming that a medical resident and a very upset patient were on the verge of exchanging blows. Hurriedly I ran to the two grown men paired off ready to bash one another. "You seem very angry," I said to the patient as calmly as possible. "You're damn right I'm angry, Dr. Pawlicki, not at you, but at this ### idiot." However, because his anger was addressed, he immediately began to calm down. The conversation turned from yelling into problem solving.

It obviously took no special training on my part to recognize that this patient was angry, but this is an example of what happens when emotions become the focus of conversation. If I say that you seem sad today or happy or whatever emotion is observed, you are likely to respond by either confirming or denying that emotion. You're then likely to expand on your feelings and we can more easily engage in a personal conversation.

Not all emotions are easy to identify. Obviously rage and anger are easy, but mild depression is much more subtle. Many emotions have a significant range. Happiness seems obvious, but people in flow, a form of deep absorption in some greatly enjoyed activity, are likely to evidence little outward pleasure but report substantial happiness later on.

Hurt is another emotion that is often less evident. Men in particular tend to camouflage hurt, since it is often associated with vulnerability, and men are acculturated to hide weakness. This is one of the reasons men are less likely to seek therapy and more likely to put off going to the doctor.

Reading another person's emotion is most often a sign of caring. For those who are unsure of the emotion there is an easy remedy.

Privately ask, "You seem sad today. Are you?" A simple question. A good means of connecting and caring. We often say we would like more close relationships. Honing your sensitivity skills is a good means of achieving that important goal.

CHAPTER 53

Boundaries: Limits needed for good relationships

I CAN'T REMEMBER the names of my elementary school teachers with the exception of Mrs. Gordon, my sixth grade teacher. I suspect that's because she had a particular form of punishment for the boys. When a boy misbehaved in Mrs. Gordon's class, she called him to the front, sat him down on a stool, tied a big pink ribbon in his hair, and encouraged the class to snicker at his mortification.

I was far from the most disruptive young boy in the class, but the embarrassment that Mrs. Gordon so effectively wielded, in even the few times I experienced it, imprinted her name on my memory. Humiliation as a weapon crosses a boundary.

Boundaries play an important role in our feeling of self-worth, confidence and sense of integrity. When a boundary is breeched we feel violated.

A child facing an authority figure or a bully often lacks the power to draw a line. It is one of the most challenging experiences of growing up. As we mature into adulthood the ability to draw boundaries is a necessary skill we must learn. Not every adult possesses this ability. When they don't, it's trouble.

I sometimes treat those who are emotionally and even physically abused, sometimes requiring contact with legal authorities. I treat those who literally allow themselves to be held hostage, sometimes by an overt threat but, more often, by an underlying belief that prevents them from taking action. Often they believe that they are doing the right thing such as being a good parent, child or spouse, but they rationalize away the abuse heaped upon them, not believing that they have a viable option to do otherwise.

Take the example of a screaming child unwilling to go to the first day of school. An over-soothing parent who gives in to the yelling child may be setting up him or herself for a more troublesome pattern. The child's anxiety may be temporarily relieved and the screaming may stop when allowed to stay home, but the parent will likely face the screaming again soon. Similar concessions can happen between adults.

Like a screaming child, an adult abusing another has perceived leverage, e.g., loss of love, financial support, etc. When a therapist hears "Yes, but" it is often this reason they give for failing to establish boundaries. Poor self-esteem on the part of the victim may also be a contributing factor. Those with poor self-esteem fear retaliatory criticism if they speak up, and this fear makes them vulnerable to even more abuse.

I have found that the inability to draw boundaries is a common element in a myriad of relationship issues and thus a factor in much anxiety and depression. Adult children can feel abused by their parents, parents may feel abused by their adult children, siblings can feel abused by each other and friends and acquaintances similarly may hurt one another.

Often, people who fail to draw boundaries have not clarified the lines that must be drawn in healthy relationships: disagreeing is OK, yelling and name calling is not; calling in the middle of night is unacceptable, during the day is not; complaining about mother endlessly is not acceptable, briefly mentioning frustrations is fine; using abusive language is unacceptable, expressing your feelings is all right.

Drawing boundaries is difficult. It is difficult, in part, because it risks a retaliatory response and therefore takes courage. Standing up for your needs does not always work, but *not* standing up for your needs virtually *never* works out. When individuals repeatedly allow themselves to accept inappropriate behavior from friends or relatives without clearly expressing their displeasure, they pay a significant price.

Exercise
On Your Path, It's Critical to Know the Boundaries

Admitting that you have allowed appropriate boundaries to be crossed is difficult. It means that you are allowing another person to take advantage of you and potentially harm you. It means that you probably have rationalized away their behavior to the detriment of your own. For example, "They're in a difficult place right now. It's not the time for me to speak up." It means that you have avoided clarifying the line that defines behaviors that are demeaning, and facing up to the fact that you need to be assertive in stating what your boundaries are.

Write out answers to the questions below:

Is there a relative, friend or acquaintance that regularly behaves in a way that makes you feel abused or insulted? Write down the person's name.

What is the behavior in question? For example: insults, foul language, demeaning of your point of view, disallowing your actions, intruding inappropriately, controlling your behavior, etc. Please list.

For each of the above behaviors that you feel are offensive write out a statement that clearly and specifically state what behaviors you would like to end. For example: "I do not like foul language. Please stop it immediately." Another example: "I feel disrespected when I am not allowed to express my opinion."

CHAPTER 54

Healthy Censorship

OUR HOUSEHOLD WENT without television for about 12 years and survived quite nicely, thank you. There were a few exceptions. We pulled a 12-inch portable TV out of the closet to watch the 9/11 tragedy after hearing about it on the radio. And we saw TV at airports, friends' homes, etc. How could we not? TV, even now in the age of the Internet, is ubiquitous.

Why would we do such an unorthodox thing? Our answer falls into the category of protecting what we put into our brains, the same way we are careful regarding what we eat. Before you assume that we are members of a cult, let me rush to say that we now own and watch TV regularly, protected, at least in our minds, by modern technology such as DVRs that allow us to circumvent extreme violence and commercialism to a large degree.

Such choices are controversial from person to person and family to family. While I avoid a diet of gratuitous violence, I would not avoid literature or serious theater in which violence is woven into the plot. Because of my professional interest in the topic of pain, I have read extensively about torture throughout history that would curl your hair. But this academic interest does not translate into a routine of watching unwarranted violence on any media. A reasonable recommendation is to monitor the type and quantity of information that potentially has a harmful effect upon your mental health.

Protecting yourself from harmful input takes some attention. Choosing to avoid extreme violence may be easy, but there may be other areas where the offending input may be difficult. For example, you may have friends or relatives whose time you may want to limit. Censoring harmful interactions from friends and relatives is every bit as important as limiting unhealthy input from the media. Your response to the following questions might indicate that some censorship may be in order.

- Do you have friends or relatives that "make your blood boil" or who send you into a funk?
- Do these same people negatively linger in your brain after you have spent time with them?
- Do you spend time wishing that you had responded differently to their conversation?
- Do you spend time thinking about what you are going to say or how you are going to handle them before you encounter them?
- Are you somewhat anxious when you know you are going to be speaking to them?

All of us can be annoying at times, but it is the deeply negative that I speak of. You may not be able to eliminate contact with those who are truly unpleasant, but you can certainly limit the time that you share in their toxic environment.

The idea, by the way, falls under another good rule of mental health — control what you can control. Treat your mind with the care you treat your body. There is a saying that "you are what you eat." My belief is that you are only as mentally healthy as what and who you allow to enter your brain and in what quantity.

CHAPTER 55

Really Knowing One Another

YOU PROBABLY KNOW a good deal about your spouse and very close friends. If you don't, you'd be wise to work on it, for the more you share, the deeper your relationships.

Connecting with others is crucial to cementing and enhancing relationships, but, even with a superficial level of knowledge, attachments can be made.

Here is a simple but dramatic example. Many years ago a young woman was admitted to our multidisciplinary chronic pain unit with severe and debilitating headaches. One day during physical therapy, she fell into a coma-like state and was unresponsive. Of course, a physician was immediately called, and onto the scene came our physical medicine and rehabilitation doctor. Fortunately this doctor had done the initial evaluation with the patient and knew her history. Two pieces of information are crucial to this story. First, the patient was a devoted Elvis Presley fan and had told the doctor. Second, our physician's avocation was Community Theater, where he starred in many productions.

Seeing the patient numb to any normal stimuli, our doctor got down on the floor and began softly singing to the young woman, "Love me tender, love me true, never let me go." And then repeating the stanza he added, "Come on, come on, sing with me — Love me tender, love me true, never let me go." To the relief and surprise of the physical therapist and other staff gathered around, the patient began to emerge from her state, singing softly, opening her eyes and becoming more lucid. A connection was made because of the doctor's comprehensive evaluation.

Hypnotists excel when they can connect to their subject in some way. A pediatric emergency room doctor and skilled hypnotist at the University of Cincinnati Children's Hospital was known to sometimes gain control of a screaming child by mimicking the child's scream. After tuning to the matching tone and volume, he would then control the scream by raising and lowering it, whereupon the child would follow his lead. In a short while, the doctor would bring the screaming to an end.

Mahatma Gandhi was a master strategist, not only in sizing up India's occupiers, the British, but exceedingly clever in gaining the support of the Indian people. Gandhi is usually pictured as a tiny man wearing a loincloth. But when he returned to India from South Africa, where he spent the early part of his life as a lawyer, he was attired in a typical British suit. A suit is unlikely to make a connection with the poor masses of India. However, a loincloth would, and did.

These three stories make an important point. When we know details about others and we connect with them in some way, we are more likely to both influence one another and maintain a lasting relationship.

A friend tells a story that illustrates how the amount of time spent with another person doesn't necessarily correlate with a deep relationship. The story is of a man who played sports with friends regularly for over 20 years and unexpectedly took his own life. Shocked by the tragedy, a friend's wife asked her husband if anyone saw this coming. The husband said, "No, not at all." The wife replied, "You were with him for 20 years and considered him a friend. What did you talk about?" "Oh", said the husband, "you know, this and that, sports, nothing special."

Nothing special, indeed!

For those people you really care about, ask questions and listen. Learn details of their lives. You'll both be the better for it.

Exercise
Knowing Your Friends in Depth is a Great Path to Happiness

It's obvious that deep relationships consist, in great part, in knowing a good deal about your relatives or friends. The more that you know and accept, the more intense the relationship is likely to be. The step to increasing the intensity of a relationship, therefore, appears fairly straightforward. If you wish to become closer to another person, carefully and sincerely elicit and listen to their life story, values and interests

Choose two relatives or friends you would like to know more deeply, and during the next two weeks write out some new information that you have learned as a result of your effort to sincerely listen to them.

Friend/relative 1

Friend/relative 2

CHAPTER 56

Invest In Friendships: The best safety net you can have

Most of us have given at least fleeting attention to our financial security, knowing that it is wise to invest early to be prepared for potential challenges later. We would do well to adopt that same philosophy for friendship. Friendship is one of those things that you can never have too much of, and its value only increases with age. It is not surprising then, that those with more and deeper friendships appear significantly happier than those without friendship. Indeed, for many, the greatest fear is to end their lives alone.

It is obvious, then, that it is important to nurture and cultivate friendships. But like the admonition to save for retirement, the suggestion to build friendships is often left to a later day. As in the financial analogy, acting now is inconvenient; it involves work and maybe even pain. The work of getting out of a regular routine, taking time and enduring social niceties, the pain of tolerating differences in style and opinion — are the little barriers that make finding and building friendships hard.

Finding a friend with whom you truly connect is difficult. The heart of friendship is trust; trust that the person will be there for you during moments of stress, trust that the friend will really listen to your needs, trust that the friend cares about you so much that he or she will temporarily sacrifice his or her needs if you are in need. Of course, there are other benefits of friendship as well — the ability to be openly frank, to laugh together and to share memories.

For some, these special friendships have just happened, a miracle of happenstance. But for most they have to develop over time. And for virtually everyone, there has been an element of work. It is the work that many avoid, the work of getting out there and making yourself available and then sticking with friends through the normal ups and downs of closeness.

Perhaps the most challenging aspect of gaining and nurturing a deep friendship is that such a relationship requires a degree of vulnerability. For a true friend knows all about you, including your faults, and still likes you. This is where men are at a disadvantage, because they are acculturated to be competitive, particularly with other men. Competition and vulnerability are polar opposites. The result is that men generally have fewer and less intense friendships than women.

Another problem is that men tend to place all of their friendship eggs in one basket, typically their wives. When tragedy strikes and the one friend is lost, the man is devastated and in a much deeper hole than those with many friends. In my opinion, this is a major contributor to the fact that men live an average of 5.2 years fewer than women.

All this is to emphasize once again the value of friendship and that gaining close friendship requires patience, perseverance, effort and work. People don't set about gathering friends to protect themselves against difficult times the way that people save money for challenging financial periods. That sounds too Machiavellian. We want friends for more lofty motives. But the two motives, future support and present enjoyment, can intertwine. Remember, friendship is mutually beneficial. When you seek out others for their friendship and long-term support, you're offering the same in return — a very good trade.

The ingredients for close friendship are quite clear — sharing time, listening, caring, being responsible, building trust through availability and reliability. Another ingredient is simply expressing a sincere interest in your friend's life. These are investments that pay the greatest dividends. They are investments in your long-term well being as well.

CHAPTER 57

Preparing for Life's Trials and Tribulations

THE OPENING LINE from the book, *The Road Less Traveled*, by Scott Peck is, "Life is difficult." He goes on to say that once you accept this fact you've taken a major step in managing life's challenges. But I'd like to suggest an additional consideration in combating life's challenges — actively pursuing happiness. Those who regularly engage in practices that increase happiness are actually preparing themselves to manage life's trials.

Our own individual list of struggles will vary, but all of us will experience a few of the following: serious illness, loss of loved ones, financial difficulties and tragedy to those around us. And no one escapes the end of life.

Since these difficulties inevitably confront us, is there anything we can do to prepare ourselves for these challenges? After much consideration I believe that the very same attitudes and practices that increase our happiness, are actually preparations for the management of the darker side of life. Let me review some of the major strategies we've already discussed:

1. **Control what you can control.** "I can only manage what's under my control, nothing more." Indeed separating what you can control from what you cannot is a fundamental aspect of good mental health and happiness. Likewise such a personal practice again sets the stage for effective management of life's greatest puzzles. Those who become bogged down with things

beyond their control are limited in their capability to experience happiness and restricted in their ability to manage suffering.

2. **I'm responsible for my happiness.** "I'm ultimately responsible for my own happiness, and I've gone through some pretty tough times." Personal responsibility and perspective are crucial to happiness and are instrumental in managing the difficult times in life. People who believe that their well being is their own responsibility tend to be happy, while those who believe there is little they can do to control their fate are far less likely to be so. When life's problems appear, individuals who consistently blame others become victims, and lose the very leverage they need to work through problems. Alternatively, those who view their problems in the larger perspective tend to do a better job of managing life's inevitable difficulties.

3. **Be kind to yourself.** "I'm not perfect, but I am a loveable person." We're constantly told to love others but just as crucial is the ability to be compassionate with ourselves, forgive our shortcomings and appreciate our strengths — wonderful skills for maintaining a strong sense of well being. When clouds cover the horizon, those who maintain greater self compassion are less prone to blame themselves. They are more likely to understand that things beyond their control are part of the vagaries of life. Such a perspective allows constructive problem solving.

4. **"I have so much to be thankful for."** Practicing gratefulness: Anecdotally and empirically it has been shown that those who are consistently grateful are happier than those who do not. When life's difficulties appear, the grateful habit expresses itself in the manner in which we focus our attention on the positives, as well as compare our difficulties with those worse off — a major tool in grappling with life's challenges.

5. **Expanding and deepening friendships** "I'm so fortunate to have so many good friends." The relationship between the number of friends we have, particularly close friendships, and happiness is strong. The same bonds play a critical role in how well we heal when tragedy hits. Those who are more alone and keep all of their sorrows inside tend to suffer longer, while those who have friends who can listen, empathize and care are more able to move on.

6. **Practice kindness to others.** "I do my best to be kind." Those who consistently go out of their way to be kind immediately gain by their action and are likely to receive reciprocal acts of caring. Such behavior deepens the very network of friendship that most of us crave which, in turn, supports us during times of stress. Kindness also strengthens our self-image and confidence, valuable assets when problems appear.

The list goes on: listening well, forgiving, volunteering, focusing on healthy internal dialog and exercising, are good practices to enhance happiness. All contribute to minimizing the emotional pain that accompanies life's challenges. I have often suggested that happiness takes work and, of course, it does. Ingredients that build a lifetime of general well being take time, energy and attention. Practice of those same attitudes and behaviors help protect and heal us during the troubling side of life as well.

You might want to mark this chapter as one to return to on a periodical basis. Following these recommendations will go a long way to keeping you on the path to happiness.

Postscript

Although writing a book is hard work, it can also be a labor of love, as is the case here. The content herein, represents my experiences, perceptions and beliefs. They are sometimes difficult for me to follow in a complicated world. Nevertheless, they have navigated me through the challenges of life as I work diligently to stay on the path that I've outlined to you. When I momentarily lose my footing, I am drawn back to these beliefs to gain my way.

Please feel free to correspond with me digitally through my website, www.robertpawlicki.com, where you'll find additional essays, speaking engagements, radio presentation information, YouTube links, and contact information. I hope to hear from you.

Acknowledgements

The chasm between the first draft and the final book can be enormous. The author's work becomes clear — run-on sentences to rein in, mangled syntax to straighten, and cherished phrases, suddenly not so profound, to be pruned. Physical and emotional energy are required to work through the red ink.

To cross such a chasm of pitfalls takes the help of many thoughtful, caring, and intelligent people and to them I am grateful.

Caring is particularly worth highlighting. It's easy to tell a friend that they look especially nice today. It's much more difficult to state what you like and dislike in their writing and then suggest an alternative. In other words, to provide constructive criticism. If the writer is willing to remain open, listen to the advice offered and judiciously apply it, writing improves and relationships deepen.

I have belonged to writer's groups whose guidelines were to give only supportive comments, a comfortable environment, perhaps, but not conducive to meaningful growth. If you are a reader of acknowledgements, you know that they reveal inevitable testimonials to strong and personal bonds between author and critics, in spite of the painful delivery of defects brought to the author's attention. Perhaps more so, because of it.

In writing this book I have had a bounty of friends, editors and readers provide me with constructive guidance that only increases my gratitude and affection for them.

First and foremost is my primary editor and wife, Gail Scarbrough. She begins the process of helping move my words from a sow's ear hopefully closer to the desired silk purse. That I supply her with an abundance of red ink helps.

I'm very fortunate to have Gayl and Dick Glover, wonderful and talented people, as friends. Gayl, with her astute eye and sharp pen, dramatically altered my early draft. Her suggestions permeate much of the final product. Dick, along with his contribution as a reader, has once again, lent his photographic and artistic skills to produce a cover that conveys the thrust of the book.

My friend of over 30 years, Doris Grieder, has provided valuable comments along with her reliable and caring support.

Readers Jennifer Messner, Marie Elaine DeAngelis, Zeddie and Carol Bowen, Joan Sedberry, Julie Harris, Marilyn Wander and Lawson Wulsin, all contributed to a clearer and more readable text.

The essays that make up this book have been previously published in the *TWATL — This Week at The Landings* — a Savannah, Georgia magazine. During the 8 years of our relationship, I have received the consistent support of publisher/editor, Jerry Sandy, and Director of Production, Pam Burgess. It has been pure pleasure to work with them. I thank them.

And to the people who read my work, who find my thoughts worth their time, thank you. When one of you tells me that you enjoy my writing or that it has changed your life, it makes my day.

Recommended Books

Books based on research data

Ben-Shahar, T., *Happier*, McGraw-Hill Books, New York, NY, 2007.

Haidt. J. *The Happiness Hypothesis*, Basic Books, New York, NY, 2002.

Gilbert, D., *Stumbling on Happiness*, Vintage Books, New York, NY, 2005.

Lyubromirsky, S., *The How of Happiness*, The Penguin Press, New York, NY, 2008.

Myers, D., *The Pursuit of Happiness*, Avon Books, New York, NY, 1992.

Rubin, G., *The Happiness Project*, HarperCollins Publisher, New York, NY, 2009.

Seligman, M., *Learned Optimism*, Alfred A. Knopf, New York, NY, 1991.

Seligman, M., *Authentic Happiness*, Free Press, New York, NY, 2002.

Seligman, M., *Flourish*, Free Press, New York, NY, 2011.

General advice books on happiness and well being

Kaufman, B., *Happiness Is a Choice*, Ballantine Books, New York, NY, 1991.

Lama, Dalai, *The Art of Happiness*, Penguin Putnum, New York, NY, 1998.

Lama, Dalai and Tutu, D. *The Book of Joy: Lasting Happiness in a Changing World*, Penguin Random House, New York, NY, 2016.

Pawlicki, R., *Success by Another Measure*, Xlibris, Philadelphia, PA, 2002.

Pawlicki, R., *Fifty Ways to Greater Well Being and Happiness: A handy and inspirational guide*, CreateSpace, Charlestown, SC, 2012.

Prager, D., *Happiness Is a Serious Problem*, HarperCollins, New York, NY, 1998.

Weiner, E., *The Geography of Bliss*, Hachett Book Group, New York, NY, 2008.

Index

About the Author

Dr. Robert Pawlicki, a retired psychologist and former University Professor, maintains a personal coaching practice, regularly teaches classes on happiness and other psychology topics, and writes a column entitled *Finding Happiness* for a Savannah, Georgia magazine.

In his professional career, he was director of the Behavioral Medicine Center at Drake Hospital in Cincinnati, Ohio, a multi-disciplinary in-patient rehabilitation program for the treatment of chronic pain patients. Dr. Pawlicki's background includes a tenured associate professorship at the State University of New York at Oswego and the rank of full professor at both West Virginia University School of Medicine and the University of Cincinnati College of Medicine. He is the author of approximately 50 research and scholarly articles as well as the books, *Success by Another Measure: Recognizing and enhancing your character* and *Fifty Ways to Greater Well Being and Happiness: A handy and inspirational guide.*

For readers who have enjoyed *Control What You Can Control: A path to Happiness*, you may want to consider my previous book, *Fifty Ways to Greater Well Being and Happiness*. The latter book received 5 stars from *Readers Favorites* and is written in the same style -– short inspirational essays that can be picked up and read as needed. The reviewer of *Readers Favorites* had this to say regarding *Fifty Ways to Greater Well Being and Happiness: A handy and inspirational guide.*

Book Review: 5 Stars

The insightful and delightful book, "50 Ways to Greater Well Being and Happiness" by Robert Pawlicki, is not your typical self-help book. The book is formatted in short paragraphs outlining fifty 'exercises' to consider when making your life happier and healthier. The book is designed to be read slowly, considering the advice within the pages and applying the ideas and principles to your own life. For example, #26 in the book, 'The Value of Stress', discusses and provides examples of how stress can actually be a positive factor in your life. When dealing with stressful situations, the author challenges us to look at these situations as 'valuable learning experiences'. Instead of looking at stress as the great big negative, stress can, in fact, make us stronger and reveal hidden abilities.

Since I adore self-help books, I was immediately drawn to the title of this book. I enjoy reading meditation-type books that give you something to consider in a few short pages. "50 Ways to Greater Well Being and Happiness" does just that. The book is full of fresh and new ideas to ponder on finding more happiness in your life. I was happy just reading this book and greatly enjoyed the different considerations that the author contributed. Although there are many books of this type and style on the market today, I was thrilled that Pawlicki offered some new refreshing insights. It is well-written and thoughtful. I felt as though I had just left my therapist's office after reading only a few of these exercises.

Readers can contact the author through his website:
www.robertpawlicki.com

Made in the USA
Middletown, DE
26 February 2018